The Ne

The
New Bike Book

How to get the
most out of your
new bicycle

Jim Langley

Illustrated by the author

Bicycle Books — San Francisco

Copyright   © James Langley, 1990

Printed in the USA

Published by   Bicycle Books, Inc
PO Box 2038
Mill Valley CA 94941
USA

Distributors to the book trade   (USA) The Talman Company, New York, NY
(Canada) Raincoast Book Distrib., Vancouver BC
(UK) Chris Lloyd Sales and Marketing Services, Poole, Dorset

Library of Congress Cataloging in Publication Data   Langley, James
The New Bike Book, How to get the most out of your new bicycle. Includes Index
1. Bicycles and Bicycling, Handbooks, Manuals, etc.
2. Authorship
I. Title

Library of Congress Catalog Card Number   89-81204

ISBN   0-933201-28-1

Table of Contents

9. Brake and Gear
Repairs 110

1. Introduction

Congratulations! You have purchased the most efficient vehicle in the world. A bicycle can cover distance with less effort from it's captain than any other machine. Whether used as a load-carrying beast of burden or for pleasure to cruise on a sunny day, if cared for, your bicycle will be a friend for life.

Use Your Bike

It has always bothered me that so many people buy bicycles and never really use them. Instead, the bike sits parked collecting dust in the garage — just a reminder of a long lost urge to exercise. I like to think that if the owner had been introduced to the bicycle in a different way, perhaps the bike would be an important part of his life.

How many potential cyclists were discouraged by their first ride? The seat was uncomfortable, the chain fell off. The tire went flat, the brakes squealed. What's wrong with this thing, they wondered. Usually very little, but it was often enough to sour the rider on the virtues of cycling permanently.

About This Book

This book is an introduction to the modern bicycle, be it a ten-speed, a cruiser or a mountain bike. It gives guidelines for fitting the bike, operating and maintaining it, basic repairs, safety and more.

The information in this book will start your relationship with the bicycle off on the right footing. I hope that it kindles a passion for the bicycle that lasts forever.

2. Today's Bicycles

Mountain bike, cruiser and ten-speed, those are the bicycle types in common use today. In the bike boom of the seventies, millions of derailleur bicycles were imported to, and sold in, the United States. These bicycles were predominantly 'racing' design ten-speeds with 'drop' (curved) handlebars, narrow saddle and lightweight wheels with high-pressure tires.

Ten-Speeds

For the bike just described, I use the term *ten-speed*, meaning any lightweight derailleur bicycle with drop handlebars. In fact, it may have ten, twelve, fifteen, even eighteen or twenty-one speed gearing. This should clear up any confusion, since most entry-level bikes of this type these days actually come with twelve speed gearing.

Cruisers

The other types of bikes mentioned here are cruisers and mountain bikes. Cruisers are distinguished from ten-speeds by their heavier frame construction and low-pressure balloon tires. Cruisers are usually equipped with wide upright handlebars, a large padded

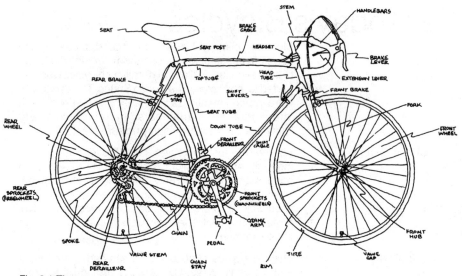

Fig. 2.1 The ten-speed bike, showing names of parts.

seat and a five- or six-speed drivetrain. Although cruisers are still available today, they are being edged

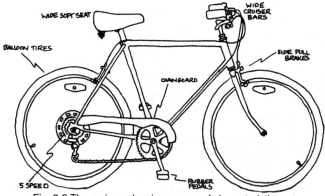

WIDE SOFT SEAT

WIDE CRUISER BARS

BALLOON TIRES

SIDE PULL BRAKES

CHAINGUARD

RUBBER PEDALS

5 SPEED

out by the mountain bike and its newer, and generally slightly less rugged and sophisticated variant, the so-called hybrid. These types of bikes will be covered in more detail in the next section below.

Fig. 2.2 The cruiser, showing names of characteristic parts.

Mountain Bikes and Hybrids

Mountain bikes, also referred to as ATB's, and hybrids are a blend of the functionality of the ten-speed and the durability of the cruiser. They are probably the most popular models available today.

These bikes offer great safety features and durability for all uses, both off-road and on the road. They come with flat handlebars with heavy duty brake levers and indexed thumb shift levers. The mountain bike rolls on

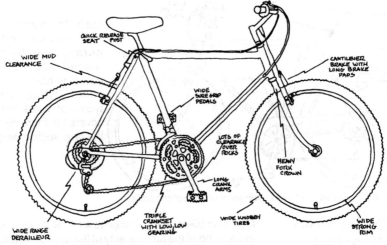

Fig. 2.3 The mountain bike, showing names of characteristic parts.

wide knobby tires for traction on all terrain types. Heavy-duty rims, reinforced frames, special brakes, and wide-range gearing make this machine exceptional for trail riding. The extra durability makes it equally suitable for the hazards of the city.

3. Setting up the Bicycle

Four adjustments to your new bicycle determine how comfortable it will be to ride: *seat height, seat angle, handlebar height* and *extension length*.

Seat Height

The seat height is the most important adjustment to make a bike easy to pedal. If the seat is too low, you risk injuring your knees when you attempt to climb steep hills or ride long distances. If the seat is too high, you risk pain in the lower back, a different type of knee problem and loss of control over your bicycle. Fortunately, it's not too difficult to find the proper seat height for most people.

Adjust the seat so your legs are completely extended with your heels on the pedals when the pedals are at the bottom of the stroke. Make this adjustment sitting on the bike with the bike in a doorway. Support yourself by holding onto the doorjamb, and pedal backwards with your heels on the pedals. The best way to establish the correct seat height is with the help of a friend. While you pedal, your friend should watch you from behind to see how you reach the pedals through

Fig. 3.1
Ball of foot over pedal axle

3.2 Seat height determination

the pedal stroke. The seat should be high enough so the knees are locked at the bottom of the pedal circle. If your friend tells you that your hips are rocking back and forth as you pedal backwards, the seat is too high. With the seat properly adjusted, you should be able to pedal backwards, heels on pedals, and keep your pelvis steady. Now you will have the correct bend in your knees when pedaling with the balls of your feet on the pedals (when you cycle you should always pedal with the balls of your feet directly over the center of the pedals).

Reaching the Ground

When the seat is adjusted to the proper height, it is difficult to put both feet on the ground when sitting on the saddle. At first this will feel awkward. Remember that the seat is adjusted to allow a comfortable, efficient leg reach to the pedals when *riding*.

Getting On and Off

To get your feet on the ground when stopped, slide forward off the seat, and you'll be able to stand, straddling the frame. If you find it difficult to mount the bike with the seat adjusted correctly, try standing over the frame first. Then put a foot on the pedal that is down and use it to push yourself up onto the seat. If you push off while you do this, the bike will roll forward and you can put your other foot on the other pedal and start riding.

Seat Angle

Start riding your bicycle with the top of the saddle level

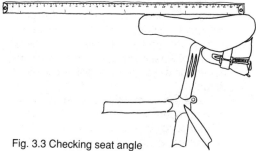

with the ground. If you have trouble determining if the seat is level, put a carpenter's level on the seat to check it. Don't have a level handy? Use a yardstick. Place it on edge on top of the saddle with twenty four inches or so extending toward the front of the bike. By looking at the yardstick and comparing it to the top tube of the bike, you can usually tell if the seat is level or

Fig. 3.3 Checking seat angle

not (assuming the bike does not have a slanted top tube — in that case, use any other horizontal plane for reference). If it's not level, loosen the bolt that fastens the saddle to the seat post and level it before tightening it again.

A Word About Seats

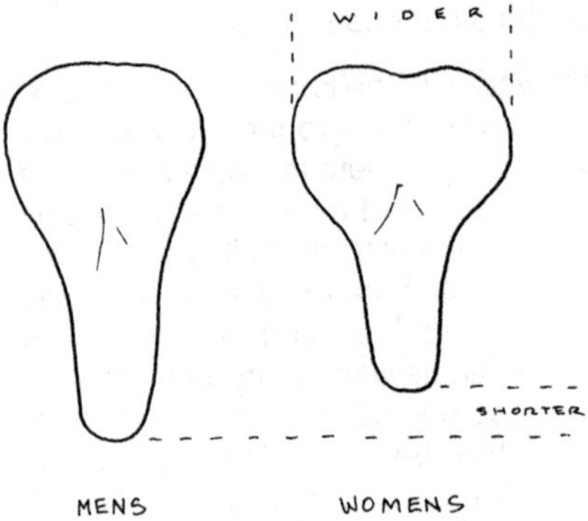

Fig. 3.4 Men's and women's seats

There are many different types of seats available. If the original one is uncomfortable, you will soon think of a bike ride as torture instead of fun. It is important to find a good seat for your new bike, so you feel good about riding. Sometimes this takes a lot of trial and error. Most shops will let customers try seats for a while to select the most comfortable model. Many riders will get used to a seat if they ride enough. However, if after a couple of weeks' riding the seat is still uncomfortable, you should look for another model.

There are so many special seats available for riders with problems that there is no reason to suffer any more. Some of the best seats are stuffed with a gel filling that

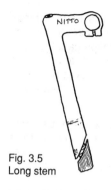

Fig. 3.5
Long stem

Handlebar Height

softens them immeasurably. Some riders prefer to try a seat cover instead of a new seat; they increase the padding on a seat.

Beware of seats that are too wide. If the seat is very wide, it can make it quite difficult to pedal efficiently. This is because the wide seat bumps the back of your thighs, preventing you from completing a good smooth pedal stroke. Wide seats can also cause chafing.

Good seats are available in two categories: women's and men's. This is a good starting point, but it is not uncommon for a man to find a woman's seat comfortable and vice versa. Trying seats out is the best way to find the right one for you.

On ten-speeds, the top of the handlebars should be one to two inches below the top of the seat. Too upright a riding position can cause pain in the lower back, because the cyclist ends up with most of his weight over the rear wheel. This can be a problem, since the narrow tires don't absorb much road shock at all.

The ideal position on a ten-speed should place you balanced between the seat, the handlebars and the pedals, each absorbing some of your body weight and cushioning some of the ride roughness. Long distance touring cyclists may want their handlebars as high as the seat on their bike. With racing type handlebars, it may be necessary to buy a special stem to be able to raise the bars as high as the top of the seat. The Nitto Technomics stem provides plenty of length for riders who need extra height.

Flat Handlebars

Cruisers and mountain bikes have wide flat bars that sometimes curve back toward the rider. This creates a more upright riding position regardless of how high or low the stem is. The upright position is fine for mountain bikes and cruisers because the big tires hold enough air to absorb some road shock and soften the ride. With most types of handlebars, you can rotate the

Fig. 3.6 Cruiser handlebars

Fig. 3.7 Mountain bike handlebars

Stem Extension

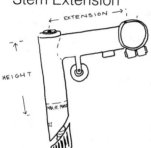

Fig. 3.8
Handlebar stem

The Fit Kit

bars inside the stem to find the best bar angle for you to grip the bars easily.

Bicycle manufacturers use different stem extensions (lengths) for the various frame sizes they offer. These sizes are intended to fit an average person who would use each frame size. If you find this brings the handlebars too close or too far, the stem can be replaced. The proper stem extension should allow you to ride with a slight bend in your elbows, regardless of where your hands are on the handlebars. If you have to lock your elbows to reach the bars, that will be a sign that the extension is too long. If it's hard to get relaxed on the bike, and you find that you are constantly pushing yourself back on the seat to feel right, it is more likely it is too short for your upper body proportions.

If you intend to ride your bike seriously for training and racing, you should consider having a professional fitting done by a bicycle shop that uses a set of fitting tools called the *Fit Kit*. Using the Fit Kit, a mechanic or sales person can accurately record your body measurements and use them with charts in the manual to determine the best frame and component sizes and optimum adjustments for your physique.

Another very important adjustment that can be done very accurately with the Fit Kit is cleat adjustment. Anyone using cleted shoes will benefit tremendously from this procedure. It guarantees that you will not damage your knees. The Fit Kit's rotational adjustment correctly positions your feet over the pedal spindle both fore and aft and laterally.

Having such a fitting done takes a while and will cost something, but if you plan to ride a lot, it will save you so much trouble that it is well worth it. If you ever decide to upgrade your bicycle, it can help in other ways. When you have a fitting done, you'll receive a chart with all your measurements on it. Also on this chart are the recommended frame and component sizes. These come in very handy when you go looking for a new bicycle or frame. You'll be able to dazzle the sales people with your professionalism, which will keep them on their toes.

Do it Yourself

If you decide not to have a professional fitting done, you can do a pretty good job yourself, following my suggestions. Should you discover that your bike proves uncomfortable adjusted as recommended, experiment with the adjustments. If necessary, it's possible to make major changes to your bike using custom equipment. It should not be painful to look forward at the road. If you develop pain in the neck, the lower back or the shoulders, you may want to customize the bicycle's fit with different parts; but expect to spend some time looking in different shops to find parts to do the trick and test them out.

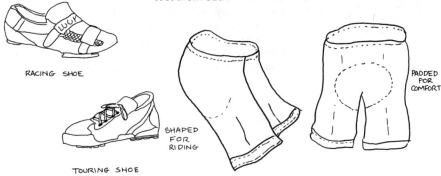

RACING SHOE

TOURING SHOE

SHAPED FOR RIDING

PADDED FOR COMFORT

Fig. 3.9 Cycling shoes   Fig. 3.10 Cycling shorts

Comfort on the Bike

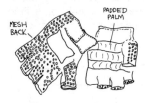

Fig. 3.11 Cycling gloves

To a degree, comfort is achieved by riding habits. Try riding standing up occasionally to get the weight off your seat, and alternate hand positions frequently to avoid numb fingers.

Cycling clothing can also go a long way toward comfort on the bike. Cycling gloves, shorts and shoes are designed to pamper the rider. They act as buffers between the cyclist and his or her bicycle. The padding on gloves protects the hands from road shock transmitted through the handlebars, and protects them from gravel in the event of a crash. Shorts are seamless and generously padded, and cycling shoes contain an internal reinforcement that helps pedaling and keeps the pedals from 'biting' the soles of your feet.

4. The Controls

To enjoy cycling, it's important you understand how to operate the bicycle safely and efficiently. The two things you need to master on a bicycle are the brakes and the gears.

Braking

The brakes don't only stop the bicycle, they also control its speed. The brake levers are located on the handlebars. The brake for the front wheel is positioned on the front fork and for the rear wheel on the brake bridge or the seat stays. The brakes are applied by queezing the levers. They press rubber pads against the wheel rims, slowing or stopping the bike. Usually the right lever operates the rear brake and the one on the left the front brake.

Braking a bicycle is not complicated. When the brakes are applied, the rider is pitched forward, transferring most of his weight onto the front wheel. It is best to brake hard with the rear brake first and then gradually apply the front brake, increasing its pressure until both front and rear brakes are equally applied. Never apply only the front brake. This mistake could throw you over the handlebars. The trick when braking hard is to avoid skidding the rear wheel. It is difficult to control the bike if the wheel locks and skids. Practice braking until you can stop effectively without skidding.

Off-Road Braking

Stopping a bike off-road can take more skill than braking on the road because of the difference in the surfaces. On dirt, the wheels will skid sooner, so it's important to practice braking, and learn the fine line between reducing the speed and skidding the wheels. If you are descending on dirt, it's best to leave the front brake alone and control speed by pumping the rear brake, i.e. increasing and decreasing lever force intermittantly. With practice, you can even use a rear wheel skid to your advantage when braking downhill around corners.

Wet Weather Braking

Use caution when braking in wet weather. Bicycle rim brakes lose most of their effectiveness in the rain. Keep the speed of the bike under control, and anticipate stops by regularly pumping the brakes. In wet weather, the rims pick up water which acts as a lubricant, reducing the grip of the brake shoes. Pumping the brake wipes the water off the rim so the brake shoes can 'grab' the rim, instead of sliding on a wet, slippery surface. In wet weather, always be prepared to stop. Remember to keep the speed of the bike down and to allow plenty of distance to stop.

Extension Levers

Fig. 4.1 Extension levers

Some ten-speeds come equipped with extension levers. These auxiliary levers are attached to the sides of the brake levers and follow the upper flat part of the handlebars. They permit the rider to put the brakes on with the hands on the tops of the handlebars. Extension levers were invented to appeal to the recreational cyclist who rides most often in an upright position, even though his bike is set up with drop handlebars.

Extension levers are sometimes called 'safety levers', but this is a misnomer if ever there was one. The levers are best thought of as an accessory on a bike. Their only use is for slowing the bike down when you are not going very fast.

They should not be used as a substitute for the main brake levers. Extension levers do not have the leverage that the main levers provide. When they are used to

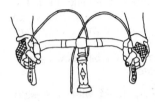

Fig. 4.2 Riding on the hoods

stop the bike, they flex enough to reduce braking power considerably. You can apply much more force with the regular levers.

Extension levers are flexible, and that's a problem when braking in an emergency, but the real problem with relying on these auxiliary levers is that you get used to riding with your hands close together on the top of the handlebars. In an emergency, this is the last place you want your hands. The wider the hands are apart, the more control the rider has over the steering of the bicycle. Practice operating the brakes with both levers, and remember to position the hands close to the regular levers when traveling at high speed. Use extension levers only on low speed recreational rides.

Riding on the Hoods

Many neophyte cyclists believe that it is necessary to ride with their hands on the lower handlebar position to operate the main brake levers. There is a very comfortable riding position that gives access to the main brake levers without having to reach so low. This position puts your hands on the top of the brake lever hoods. Straddle the top of the main lever with the thumb and forefinger, and wrap the fingers over the lever or around the lever hood. This places the levers under the fleshy part of the hand. The fingers wrap over the front of the brake lever, and the bike can be slowed or stopped without bending to reach the drops by tipping the wrist and squeezing the lever. Rubber hoods on the brake levers help make this position more comfortable.

Shifting

The primary difference between a derailleur equipped bike that has ten or more speeds and a three-speed or one-speed bicycle is the transmission. Derailleur bicycles are equipped with a drivetrain that permits the rider to adjust the bicycle's pedal resistance to exactly suit the terrain. Used properly, the gears on a modern lightweight bicycle offer tremendous possibilities for travel. A fit cyclist can easily travel fifty to seventy five miles a day if he or she uses the gears skillfully.

Learning to Shift

The only way to learn how to shift a bicycle is to practice. You have to continue pedaling while shifting, so it can be tricky at first. The chain seems to be slipping underfoot and makes some ominous noises; but don't worry: it's unlikely you'll damage a bicycle by shifting gears.

Index levers, sometimes called clicking levers, are installed on most new bicycles these days. These have set positions built in for each gear, so the rider simply clicks the lever into the desired position and the derailleur moves to the correct gear. If you are new at shifting, index levers are fantastic. As long as you remember to ease off your pedal pressure while shifting, you'll have a perfect shift every time.

Index Shifters

It used to be difficult to learn how to shift a derailleur-equipped bicycle. Their *friction* shift levers did not automatically find the gear for you. With this type of shifters, it was necessary to feel the gear with your feet as you slowly moved the lever and pedaled gently. Even expert riders occasionally had to look back at the chain and freewheel to see what gear they were in, and to watch for a smooth shift. If your bike is set up with friction shift levers, don't despair: It takes practice to use these levers initially, but they are every bit as reliable as index levers and will shift the gears just fine.

It is possible to install index levers on any bicycle if you decide you'd prefer their shifting help. If you want to do this, you will have to buy more than just the levers, so be prepared to spend some money. The best thing to do is to take your bike to a bike shop and ask for advice about part availability and cost.

How Shifting Works

The bicycle is shifted with levers mounted on the frame, on the handlebars or on the handlebar stem. The shift levers have cables attached to them. Pulling or pushing the lever moves the cable. The cables are attached to mechanisms called derailleurs, and when the rider moves the shifter, the derailleur moves sideways, exerting pressure on the chain. As long as the rider is pedaling, the chain will follow the derailleur sideways onto a different sprocket.

If you look at the path of the chain on your bicycle, you'll see that it runs over round toothed sprockets. Near the pedals there are two or three big sprockets, referred to as chainrings. On the hub of the rear wheel there are five, six, seven

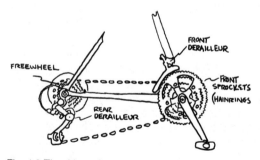

FRONT DERAILLEUR

FREEWHEEL

FRONT SPROCKETS (CHAINRINGS)

REAR DERAILLEUR

Fig. 4.3 The drivetrain

or perhaps even eight smaller sprockets. Most cruisers only have one front chainring, usually providing five or six gears.

The right hand lever controls the rear derailleur. With it you select which of the sprockets on the rear you need. The left lever controls the front derailleur. With this lever you select which of the chainrings you need.

When shifting the rear derailleur, the larger the sprocket the chain is on, the easier it is to pedal. For climbing hills, the larger rear sprockets are used. On the front it's the opposite. The smaller the chainring, the easier it is to pedal; the larger the chainring, the harder it is.

Constant Pedaling Speed

Derailleur bicycles are not shifted like automobiles. You don't start off in first, then shift into second, then third as you pick up speed. You try to keep a constant pedaling speed and then shift whenever your legs are working too hard or spinning too fast.

Shifting the right lever makes small differences in how hard or easy it is to pedal. Usually, you shift one sprocket at a time and on the rear sprockets the size does not vary greatly from one sprocket to the next.

Whenyou shift one sprocket up or down, it will get a little easier or harder to pedal. Shifting the left lever will make a greater difference: usually, there is a bigger difference between the sizes of the chainrings, so shifting makes a major change in pedal effort.

Cadence

The rider is the engine that propels the bike. Accomplished cyclists try to maintain a steady pedaling speed, usually between sixty and one hundred revolutions per minute. This pace is called *cadence*. Pedal revolutions are counted on one pedal only if you use a watch and count.

It's easiest to learn cadence using a bicycle computer. These handy accessories inform the cyclist about his speed, distance and on many models cadence. As the road varies in ups and downs, head winds and tail winds, the pedaler shifts gears regularly every time the pedal speed slows down or speeds up noticeably. This monitoring of pedaling speed is the gauge by which the rider checks the selected gear. A faster pedaling speed is better for riding because it minimizes fatigue and develops supple leg muscles. Pedaling slowly, pushing hard in big gears, is the worst approach to cycling. It will only lead to sore legs and usually knee damage. Learning to pedal correctly (a fast, or high, cadence) is the first step towards becoming an effective cyclist. The higher pedaling speed lets you dance over hills and ride long distances without straining.

Practice Shifting

To practice shifting, find a parking lot with little or no traffic and ride around in circles, shifting gears. With index shifting it won't take long to master this art. Some index bikes have an indexed derailleur in the front as well as in the rear. Most bikes, however, have indexing only on the rear derailleur, so it is still necessary to learn to shift the front derailleur.

Triple Chainrings

On triple chainring bikes, it takes some skill to find the gear you want, positioning the front derailleur so the chain is not grinding the side of it. As you ride around, shift the front derailleur, and watch it between your feet. Practice smooth shifts with light pedal pressure. Wait for the chain to engage the next sprocket before putting more pressure on the pedals.

Shift the rear derailleur and watch how the chain

moves closer to one side or the other of the front derailleur cage as you shift up and down the gears on the rear cluster. This is an important part of shifting the gears: If you let the chain rub against the side of the front derailleur, you'll wear out the front derailleur eventually. Most new riders hear the grinding noise but are not sure how to correct it. All it takes is moving the front derailleur a little bit away from the chain. This is called *trimming* the derailleur. You're not shifting with the derailleur, you're just changing its position to clear the chain.

Friction Shifters

A practice session is really important if you are learning to shift a derailleur bicycle equipped with standard friction shift levers. Ride around the parking lot shifting the rear derailleur. Watch the chain shifting up and down the freewheel. You can see the chain by looking back, sighting between your right leg and the bicycle. Practice shifting until you get the feel for finding one gear at a time.

The bike will let you know if you're not exactly in gear. The chain will make a chattering sound if the derailleur is not positioned correctly. It should be quiet when the bike is in gear — so if it chatters, you need to fine tune your gears by moving the shift lever a tiny bit.

Light Pedal Pressure

Whether you have index or friction shifting on your bike, you should remember that the most important part of shifting a derailleur is to use light pedal pressure during the shift. Even racers in the middle of competition ease the pressure off the pedals when they shift.

When in gear, you can pedal as hard as necessary, but you should relax the pressure while changing gears. For example, when you are pedaling hard on a hill, you should shift *before* it gets steep. If you should get stuck on a steep hill in a gear that is too hard to pedal, it's best to pedal hard a couple of times in that gear to get the speed up, then make the shift onto the next cog quickly while pedaling lightly. Sometimes you have to zigzag across the road to accomplish a shift under these circumstances, but with practice you can do it. It's always easier to pedal up a hill than to walk.

A Shifting Example

You roll down the road on a calm spring day. Pedaling the bike one revolution per second seems easy on the level blacktop. The chain is on the small chainring in the front and the middle rear sprocket. The road turns and starts to go up. It's not too steep yet, so you shift the rear derailleur into the next larger rear sprocket with the right lever (on a ten-speed they are pulled back,while the thumb shifters on mountain bikes are pushed forward to shift onto a larger sprocket).

As the hill gets steeper, you pull the right lever back all the way, shifting onto the largest rear sprocket, and climb over the top of the hill. As you start down the other side, you try to pedal but find the gear is so easy you can't keep up with the bike. Shifting the right lever up, you move the chain down a sprocket, but the change still is not big enough. You could keep shifting with the right lever, but it would be easier to shift the front derailleur lever, moving the chain onto the large chainring. This makes a big difference, and now you can pedal down the hill.

No sooner do you reach the bottom of the hill, then you start up another hill and lose all momentum. You need an easy gear quickly or you'll practically stop. You shift onto the smaller front sprocket. This gets you most of the way up the hill, but it will be necessary to shift into an easier rear sprocket to make it to the top.

The road finally levels out, and you find the gear so easy your legs are spinning like mad to ride at a good pace. You shift the rear derailleur onto the next smaller sprocket, which makes a difference, but it's still too easy, so you shift onto an even smaller rear sprocket. The chain is making a lot of noise, but the bike is definitely in gear. Looking down, you notice that the chain is close to the front derailleur cage. You move the left lever a little to center the cage of the front derailleur. With the bike running quietly and your legs pedaling comfortably, you ride into the sunset.

Gear Charts

A gear chart will help you calculate the gearing on your bicycle if you are interested in knowing exactly which gear is which. Each sprocket on the front and rear has a different number of teeth. To use a gear chart, count the number of teeth on each of the front chainrings and on each of the rear sprockets. Find each number in the appropriate column on the gear chart and circle it. Then follow each of these columns, and circle each number on the chart that coincides with your rear sprockets. The numbers on the gear chart represent the size of the gear. The larger the number, the harder the gear

Fig. 4.4 Gear chart

FREEWHEEL
(rear sprockets)

CHAINWHEELS (front sprockets)	13	14	15	16	17	18	19	20	21	22	23	24	25	26	27	28	30
26	54	50	47	44	41	39	37	35	33	32	31	29	28	27	26	25	23
28	58	54	50	47	44	42	40	39	36	34	33	32	30	29	28	27	25
30	62	58	54	51	48	45	43	41	39	37	35	34	32	31	30	29	27
32	66	62	58	54	51	48	45	43	41	39	38	36	35	33	32	31	30
34	71	66	61	57	54	51	48	46	44	42	40	38	37	35	34	33	31
41	85	79	74	69	65	62	58	55	53	50	48	46	44	42	41	40	37
42	87	81	76	71	67	63	60	57	54	52	49	47	45	44	42	41	38
45	93	87	81	76	72	68	64	61	58	55	53	51	49	47	45	43	41
46	96	89	83	78	73	69	65	62	59	57	54	52	50	48	46	44	42
47	98	91	85	79	75	71	67	63	60	58	55	53	51	49	47	45	42
48	100	93	86	81	76	72	68	65	62	59	56	54	52	50	48	46	43
50	104	96	90	84	79	75	71	68	64	61	59	56	54	52	50	48	45
52	108	100	94	88	83	78	74	70	67	64	61	59	56	54	52	50	47

$$\frac{\text{FT. SPROCKET}}{\text{RR. SPROCKET}} \times \text{WHEEL DIAM.} = \text{GEAR INCHES}$$

GEAR FORMULA

GEAR CHART
FOR 27 & 700C WHEELS
and
BALLOON TIRE (26×2.125)

GEAR INCH NUMBERS REPRESENT THE INCHES TRAVELLED PER ONE REVOLUTION OF PEDALS IN THAT GEAR. EXAMPLE:

IN A 52/13 YOU TRAVEL 108 INCHES FOR ONE PEDAL REVOLUTION *

* ACTUALLY, IN ORDER TO CALCULATE THE <u>EXACT</u> DISTANCE TRAVELLED FOR ONE REVOLUTION ITS NECESSARY TO MULTIPLY THE GEAR INCH NUMBER BY 3.14. USUALLY THE GEAR INCH NUMBERS ARE USED TO COMPARE SHIFT SEQUENCES.

and the smaller the number, the easier.

Transfer the numbers from the gear chart to a piece of paper as in the example. Be sure to put down the front and rear sprocket numbers and keep them arranged in two or three columns and however many rows as you have rear sprockets. Find the smallest number (the easiest gear) and put a one next to it. Find the next smallest number and put a two next to it, and so on, through all the gears. Now, looking at the chart, you can identify your gears from easiest to hardest.

Gear Calculation

It's not necessary to use a gear chart to figure out your gearing. You can calculate your own gear selection by counting the number of teeth on your sprockets and using the following formula for each possible combination: LARGE SPROCKET divided by SMALL SPROCKET multiplied by the WHEEL DIAMETER. An example: 42/14 x 27 = 81. If you have 700 C wheels, use 27 as the multiplier; with 26" wheels, use 26 and so on.

You don't need to fully understand your gears to shift your bike effectively. It's nice to know what gears you have, and some riders actually make a little gear chart of their ratios and tape it to their stem to refer to while

Fig. 4.5 Gear calculation

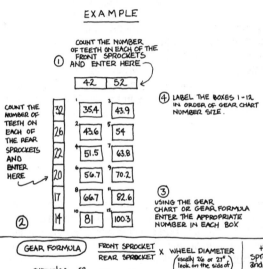

EXAMPLE

① COUNT THE NUMBER OF TEETH ON EACH OF THE FRONT SPROCKETS AND ENTER HERE

| 42 | 52 |

COUNT THE NUMBER OF TEETH ON EACH OF THE REAR SPROCKETS AND ENTER HERE

32	1 35.4	3 43.9	
26	2 43.6	5 54	
22	4 51.5	7 63.8	
20	6 56.7	9 70.2	
17	8 66.7	11 82.6	
14	10 81	12 100.3	

②

④ LABEL THE BOXES 1-12 IN ORDER OF GEAR CHART NUMBER SIZE.

③ USING THE GEAR CHART OR GEAR FORMULA ENTER THE APPROPRIATE NUMBER IN EACH BOX

GEAR FORMULA $\dfrac{\text{FRONT SPROCKET}}{\text{REAR SPROCKET}} \times$ WHEEL DIAMETER (usually 26 or 27" look on the side of the tire)

example: $\dfrac{52}{14} \times 27 = 100.3$

CUSTOM GEARING ?

IT'S POSSIBLE TO CHANGE THE GEARING ON ANY BICYCLE. IF WHEN CALCULATING GEARS THERE ARE SEVERAL DUPLICATE GEAR NUMBERS, IT WOULD BE PRACTICAL TO CHANGE A SPROCKET OR TWO TO EVEN OUT THE GEAR RANGE.

ANOTHER GOOD REASON TO CHANGE GEARING IS TO GET AN EASIER GEAR. IF YOU DISCOVER ITS VERY DIFFICULT TO GET UP HILLS YOU MAY WANT TO PUT A LOWER GEAR ON THE BICYCLE.

NOTE: Its important not to ride in gears that create a bad chain angle. Two gears that should be avoided are the large front sprocket and the large rear sprocket combination and the small front sprocket and small rear sprocket combination. These are "crossover" gears and riding in them will prematurely wear the chain and sprockets.

riding. What really matters is not whether you know which ratio you are in, but whether you know when to shift and how to find the right gear when you need it. This comes more from experience than from studying gear charts and calculations.

The important thing is to shift down anytime the pedaling is too difficult, up when it is too easy. Never lug your engine, because you may injure your knees. If the gear is comfortable, you are OK. If you discover after some practice that the gears are not adequate for the terrain — that you are struggling uphill in too hard a gear or you spin out too easily riding downhill — you may then get interested in gear charts and ratios, determining how to customize your drivetrain to make riding more enjoyable.

Crossover Gears

There are a couple of gear combinations left unused on any derailleur bike. These are the combinations that place the chain in a bad position and create excessive wear and tear on the drivetrain components. These combinations are called *crossover gears*. The two gears to avoid are the big-big gear combination (large front and large rear) and the little-little gear (small front

LITTLE/LITTLE

**TOP
VIEW**

BIG/ BIG

Fig. 4.6 Crossover gears

and small rear). Of these two gears, the latter is the worse to use. It's not really a matter of life and death whether or not you use these gears. The bike won't suddenly fall apart or anything like that. However, used over a long period, the chain and the sprockets will wear a lot faster than normal, and you will experience things like skipping of the chain.

Skipping Gears

Skipping is a problem caused by riding in the small small combination too much. What happens is that the chain wears out the teeth on the smallest freewheel cog, and when you stand up or pedal hard in that gear, the chain rides up, off the teeth and jumps forward a tooth. To the rider this is a very annoying glitch in the pedal stroke. Skipping can only be repaired by replacing the worn sprocket and sometimes the chain. If the crossover gears are avoided as much as possible this type of wear can be retarded.

New Mountain Bike Shifters

The latest mountain bikes are equipped with shifters mounted under the handlebars that accommodate the natural position of your thumb. These new shifters are made up of two closely spaced buttons on each side of the handlebars. Pressing the lower button shifts the chain onto a larger sprocket or chainring, while pressing the top button moves it to a smaller one

The beauty of this set-up is that you never have to lift your thumb above the bar to shift, and this allows you to maintain a good grip on the handlebars while shifting. It's even possible to brake and shift simultaneously.

Fig. 4.7 Under-the-handlebar shifters

5. Bicycling Safety

Riding a bicycle is simple enough. Once you learn to operate the brakes and the derailleurs, it would seem you've mastered the machine. However, there are a few other things to know before venturing onto the highways of the world. As far as traffic laws go, a bicycle is a vehicle and is required to obey all the rules of the road that apply to automobiles. Bicycles belong on the road with traffic and should not be ridden on sidewalks.

Ride on the Right

One of the leading causes of deaths among cyclists in the United States is riding against traffic. Never ride facing traffic. ALWAYS RIDE ON THE RIGHT WITH TRAFFIC! To ride against traffic is suicidal. When you ride against traffic, cars turning onto the road from driveways and intersections are apt not to see you. Drivers turning right onto a road look left and pull out into the road when it looks clear. If you ride on the left, facing traffic, every car entering the road is an accident waiting to happen.

I believe people got the idea that you cycle towards traffic because it is recommended that pedestrians should do so. On a bicycle it is a big mistake. The first step to safe riding is to ride with traffic on the right side of the road.

Obey Traffic Rules

Other rules for accident-free riding is to stop for red lights and stop signs, to signal turns, and to obey the rules of the road just as if you were driving a car. You just can't go zipping through intersections, oblivious to the signal lights. If you're lucky, you may never get hit by a car, but there's a good chance that someday you will cause an accident, and even if *you* don't get hurt, someone else will — and you'll be responsible.

Signaling

Signaling turns and stops when riding is a courtesy to other road users. It makes good sense to let motorists know what you are going to do. You'll make friends if you let others know when it's safe to pass on narrow roads, and you'll be less likely to have an accident if you let following drivers know which direction you plan to turn at an intersection.

This is an easy thing to do if you practice and get in the habit of helping other road users understand you. It's just a matter of sticking your arm out to get the driver's attention and pointing out your planned move.

If you can manage to look the driver in the eye, you can be sure he'll let you make your turn; he may even help you by blocking other traffic so you have time to get through a tight spot.

Leave Yourself an Out

Of course it's important to look out for yourself too. Often drivers try to pass on narrow roads and get very close to you. Always leave yourself an out. When riding in dangerous situations, such as over a bridge or on a narrow country lane, take the lane! Let following drivers know that the road is too narrow to pass, by riding toward the center of the lane.

Should a stubborn motorists decide to pass anyway, you'll be able to move right. Most drivers will wait, because they realize that you are blocking the lane until it widens. It helps to put your left arm out with an open palm facing back to warn the motorists that it is not safe to pass at the moment. As soon as the road widens, wave the cars past as you move as far to the right as is safe.

This maneuver is used when traffic is moving slightly faster than you are, as is usually the case on nice bicycling roads. Do not interfere with traf-

Fig. 5.1 Traffic sings and rules apply to cyclists too

fic if the average automobile speed is two or three times your speed. Some roads with high speed limits are built with generous shoulders, but not all of them. I recommend not riding on roads with high speed limits and minimal shoulders; there is too much chance for catastrophe to cyclists on this type of road.

Road Hazards

Bicycle riding can be hazardous. Even accomplished riders occasionally fall. Road conditions affect the handling of the bicycle. Use caution on sand, gravel or broken pavement, especially in corners. When it's raining, keep the speed of the bike under control and use great care in turns. On a rainy day the pavement will be most slippery when it is just getting wet. It's not nearly as bad in a downpour, because heavy rain will wash the oil off the road. Light rain and drizzle will just leave the oil sitting on the surface of the road, waiting to topple an unlucky cyclist.

I crashed in a corner on a rainy day and fell hard. I never saw the oil slick, but it was there, and I lost control because I went into the corner a little too fast and leaned my bike too far. One second I was thinking about my swell morning ride, and the next moment I was recovering in the road. I learned my lesson: in the thousands of miles since that accident, I have not crashed in the rain again, because I am very cautious. You should be too.

Mud, Sand and Railroads

Rain can turn dirt roads into mud roads. It's very tricky to handle a bike in mud. Turning can cause the front wheel to plow into the mud. Similar things happen in sand. Instead of riding and steering the bike normally, 'ski' your bike. Try to ride the bike by leaning it. To keep the front wheel from sticking in the mud or sand, sit back on the seat and apply your weight to the seat and the rear wheel instead of the front wheel.

The best way to learn how to control a bike in mud and sand is to practice, practice, practice. It's fun to learn, and not very dangerous, because you won't be going fast and the ground will be pretty soft.

Railroad tracks can jump out and grab cyclists. That may sound far fetched, but it can seem that way if you crash innocently crossing some tracks. Your best chance to cross tracks safely is to approach them at a ninety-degree angle. Straight across is the only way to get across safely every time. If you try to cross them anywhere near parallel, chances are the tracks will grip your wheel and knock you down. This is especially true in the rain, because the steel tracks are very slick when wet.

Fatigue

A lot of bicycle accidents occur because the rider is tired. Keep your rides within distances appropriate to your fitness level. Cycling takes energy. Riders lose body moisture breathing and perspiring. On long rides, carry one or two water bottles and sip every ten minutes. There's always a breeze riding a bicycle, so you will not notice that you may be dehydrated.

Food and Drink

Drink before you feel thirsty. You don't have to drink water if you prefer something tastier, but water will do a lot more for you than sugary and carbonated drinks. There are many energy drinks that contain important minerals and nutrients to refuel your system available at many bike shops and natural food stores.

Carry some food, or at least enough money to buy some. Bicycle jerseys are special shirts with pockets sewn in the back to carry food on rides. Some riders like to carry a handlebar bag stocked with food to munch on during a ride. Eating and drinking on the bike will help prevent exhaustion that can cause wobbly bike handling and poor judgment.

The Bonk

Severe energy depletion is known as the *bonk*. It's an awful feeling. Depending on how long you ride without nourishment, the feeling can vary from a light head to dizzy spells, nausea and a feeling of pins and needles in your hands and arms.

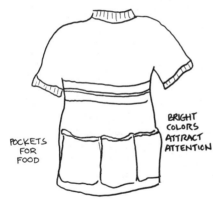

BRIGHT COLORS ATTRACT ATTENTION

POCKETS FOR FOOD

Fig 5.2 Use cycling jersey to carry food

It's an interesting phenomenon. You can rest on a bicycle because the bicycle supports you as you go. When fatigue sets in, you can rest by coasting until you feel ready to pedal again, consequently, it's possible and common for riders to push themselves too hard and bonk. In fact, it's possible to continue riding a bike long after your legs would fail to hold you up if you got off the bike and tried to stand! The bonk makes it very difficult to control your bike and exercise good judgment. The best plan is to prevent getting it in the first place by eating enough when riding.

Group Cycling

Riding with groups is great fun but presents new hazards to a cyclist. Communication between riders in a group is very important. It's best to ride single file, so the person in front can alert following riders to hazards in the road by pointing at the obstacle and shouting out what it is.

The last rider should let the people in front know when a vehicle is passing, especially if it's a bus, truck or other wide vehicle. Many accidents in groups happen over confusion in directions. Make sure everyone knows where the ride is going, so when you enter a turn no one swerves into someone else. A good plan is for the leading rider to call out a turn and point the direction.

Helmets

Now that you're terrified to ride around the block, understand that the majority of accidents result in minor scrapes. To make sure nothing more serious happens, it's a great idea to wear a helmet. A bicycle helmet will protect the most fragile part of your anatomy in a crash.

Cuts and scrapes, even broken bones, will heal, but head injuries can be very serious. A helmet practically guarantees that your head will be OK in a fall. There's really no excuse not to wear a helmet anymore. Modern cycling helmets are light, cool and stylish. If you always wear a helmet and ride carefully, the chances are good you'll never suffer a really serious injury on the bike.

Fig. 5.3 Cycling Helmet

6. Maintenance

A Bad Reputation

It's unfortunate, but derailleur bicycles have taken a bum wrap. Many, many potential owners decided not to buy ten-speed derailleur bikes because they believed them to be spindly, fragile machines. People believe the more gears a bike has, the more trouble it will be, so they opt not to buy a ten-speed.

Junk Bikes

The reputation for problems with these machines was created by the number one bike seller in the country: the department store. Department stores sell more bikes than any other two wheeler dealer. This is a shame because they typically sell only the poorest quality bicycles and don't have the knowledge or expertise to assemble them correctly, or service them when they fall apart, as inevitable they do. And these poor quality bikes have given all ten-speeds a bad reputation.

The department store wants a bike that costs them next to nothing, so they can double their cost but still sell it cheaply. Once a bike is sold, they hope to never see it again. They're not interested in stocking parts for their bikes, servicing or guaranteeing them. All they want is a quick profit. In the bike boom years of the early seventies and since, millions of department store bikes were sold. The average life of these bicycles was one year — if they were ridden at all. Most people wound up so frustrated with the shifting, braking and pedaling of the bike that they stopped riding it and decided ten-speeds weren't for them. These bikes were never fit to the riders, and they were never adjusted to work properly.

Bike Shops

Actually, any ten-speed, even the poorest quality department store bicycle, would run trouble-free, provided it was tuned by a good bicycle mechanic early in it's life. When a cycle is purchased at a bike shop, it is carefully assembled at the shop, test ridden and fit to the customer. If there are problems with it, there is a mechanic to solve them. Even used bikes often come with a guarantee. Bicycle shops want customers to enjoy riding their bicycles. It's the best place to buy a bicycle and to have it serviced.

Proper Service

If you have a bicycle that's not new and in questionable condition, take it to a bicycle shop for service. The mechanic will be happy to recommend services that the bike needs and estimate the cost. Once the bicycle is serviced, it will operate well for years if minor care is used by the owner.

Tune-Ups

Once a year it's good to take your bike to the shop for a tune-up. Tune-ups include lubrication, checking tires, adjusting brakes and gears, replacing worn or broken parts, truing wheels, adjusting bearings, tightening loose nuts and bolts, and repairing any specific problems mentioned by the owner. If a bike is ridden regularly, it will need fresh grease in the bearings and an overall check of the main components every couple of years,. Mountain bikes ridden hard under off-road conditions, may need fresh grease every six months. Riding through mud and water can quickly dissolve the grease in components.

Other than these visits to the shop, and repairs due to accidents, a bicycle needs only minor maintenance that can be performed by the owner.

Basic Owner Maintenance

The most frequent maintenance a derailleur bicycle requires is pumping up the tires. Lightweight bicycles roll easily because they are equipped with high-pressure, low-rolling-resistance tires.

Tire Pressure

The recommended pressure to inflate the tires to is marked somewhere on the side of the tire. Sometimes it is printed on a label, but often it is molded into the sidewall.

Ten-speed tires generally take 75 to 115 pounds pressure. This sounds like a lot of air to put in a skinny bicycle tire, especially when you consider that car tires take only 25 to 35 pounds. The volume of air in the car tire is greater and the pressure is less. The bike tire has high pressure but low volume. The high-pressure tires roll beautifully, as long as they are kept at recommended pressure.

It's necessary to check tire pressure regularly, because high pressure bicycle tires lose air. In the course of a week, an average ten-speed could lose twenty to forty pounds of pressure. The tire does not actually hold any air. Inside the tire is a rubber tube. It's actually the tube that leaks air. There's nothing wrong with it, it's just the nature of a tube to very slowly lose air. If the tire deflates completely overnight or when riding, there's probably a hole in the tube, but slowly losing air over a week or more is normal.

Fat Tires

Balloon tires, the tires common on cruisers and mountain bikes, take less pressure than ten-speed tires. The balloon tire was created to act as a shock absorber for the rider. On cruisers, balloon tires take twenty five to fifty pounds pressure; on mountain bikes that may be more. Riding in the woods with less air will help you control the bike over rough ground. On pavement it will make pedaling easier if you increase the pressure. Usually, balloon tires do not need to be pumped up as frequently as ten-speed tires. The lower pressure and the larger volume of balloon tires means the air won't leak out quickly.

Serious riders pump tires up just about every day. Proper tire pressure makes it easier to pedal a bicycle, so you will save energy riding on fully inflated tires. They also help prevent rim damage on rough roads. When the wheels go through a pot hole with soft tires, the edges of the hole compress the tire. Under-inflated tires can compress completely on abrupt road hazards and the wheel's rim will take the full force of the impact and get damaged.

Rims not only support the tire, but are also the surface the brakes rub on. When a rim is bent, it makes it difficult to make a good brake adjustment. To avoid rim damage, check your tire pressure regularly and try to bypass pot holes, curbs and other dangerous obstacles. If you can't avoid a hazard, at least take some weight off the wheel by getting off the saddle in a jockey's position. Riding over a pot hole off the seat with your knees and elbows bent, you can cushion the wheel's force over the obstacle and protect the rims.

Pressure Gauges

Use a tire pressure gauge to check tire pressure. Bicycle pressure gauges are not the same as automobile types. Car air gauges only go to fifty pounds or so; consequently, they're not very useful on high-pressure bicycle tires.

Home Pumps

Since you need to pump up the tires frequently, you may want to buy a bicycle pump with a built-in tire gauge. With a good pump, it's easy to inflate the tires every couple of rides. Besides protecting the rims from damage, proper tire inflation will increase tire life. Under-inflated tires have a tendency to crack prematurely and puncture easily.

Gas Station Pump Hazards

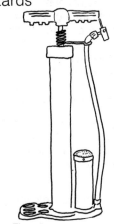

Fig. 6.1 Floor pump

Gas stations have air hoses, and it's cheaper to use them than to buy a bicycle pump. However, there are risks. The gas station hose is connected to a powerful compressor designed to put out enough air to fill a high-volume car tire quickly. The gas station pump pushes air into the tire so quickly that in three seconds it will exceed maximum pressure, sometimes blowing the tire and tube off the rim. Even if the gas station attendant pumps the tire up for you, the same may happen. Sometimes the tires will be OK for most of the day and then blow up.

An over-inflated tire can gradually creep off the rim, so you might be enjoying a downhill ride when it decides to blow up. This can be very dangerous. You cannot trust gas station air gauges that are built into the machine either. Even if you set the correct pressure, in most cases the gas station pump will continue to put air into your tire beyond the tire's capacity. Use a bicycle pressure gauge when filling tires at a gas station, and hold the hose on the valve for a couple of seconds at a time and then check it. By carefully regulating the pressure, and increasing it slowly, you can safely pump up bicycle tires at a gas station.

Lubrication

A bicycle is a machine with many moving parts. In order to keep the machine operating smoothly and quietly, it's smart to lubricate it occasionally. How often you lube your bike depends on the amount you ride it. Certain signs are an indication that the bicycle needs lubrication. A squeaky chain is a sure sign and hard-to-operate brake and shift levers is another.

When parts are dry, they wear fast and can rust. Lubricate the chain every two weeks with a spray lubricant. There are lots of different brands available that will do the job. The important thing is not to put grease or heavy oil on a bicycle chain. Heavy lubricants will lube the chain, but they will quickly pick up dirt and other road gunk and gum up the bicycle's drivetrain. A spray lube is clean, easy to use and has superior penetrating qualities to oil or grease. It can get inside the links and rollers of the chain and thoroughly lubricate it.

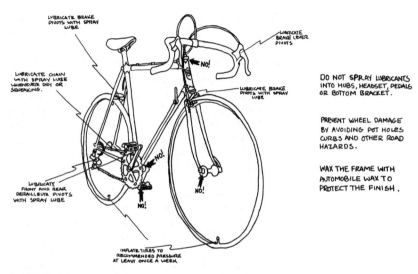

Fig. 6.2 Maintenance points

Spray lubricants are also excellent for derailleurs and brakes because of their penetrating abilities. Lots of components on the bicycle are made up of small parts moving against each other. Spray lube applied to these pivot points will help them operate freely. Use caution when spraying brake pivots. If you spray too much lube, it can spread onto the rims, ruining the braking. Never spray lube into parts containing ball bearings either: Avoid spraying directly into pedals, headset, hubs or bottom bracket. Spraying components that roll on ball bearings dissolves out the grease in these parts and will make them operate poorly and wear out early. These parts were intended to run on greased ball bearings. The grease lasts thousands of miles, provided it's not broken down by spray lubes.

Cosmetics

Bicycles are painted for protection from corrosion. Some parts are chrome-plated steel and other parts are anodized aluminum, but every part has a protective finish to protect it from rust and corrosion. Maintaining this protective finish is primarily a matter of waxing and polishing it now and then. The paint on a bicycle frame is going to get chipped sooner or later. Chips are a cosmetic, not a structural flaw. Paint chips should be touched up soon so the frame won't rust. It would take years for a chipped frame to rust all the way through, but eventually rust could ruin the frame if left unchecked long enough.

Paint Touch-up

Touching up paint jobs can be difficult. The original paint color is a combination of a primer coat and a couple of finish coats. If the bike has weathered, the color has also faded. Even if you find the exact touch-up color from a bike shop, the chances are good it won't match exactly, unless you use the same primer and apply the color coat carefully. Of course, it's not necessary to match the original color to protect the frame, but if it's an exact match you want, here are a few ideas:

Fingernail paints are available in many exotic colors, and with creative mixing, they can be made to match some flashy bicycle colors. For more conventional colors, you can try model paint. A good touch-up artist can mix paints for a perfect color match. Whatever you use for touch-up paint, it should match the chemical composition of the original paint. Some paints will attack other types of paint. Experiment on a part of the bike that is out of sight to ensure that the touch-up is compatible with the paint on the bike.

Apply the touch-up paint with a brush suited to the job. Tiny chips are easiest to fill with a tiny brush. Put a small drop of touch-up on the exposed area and spread it out to a thin coat over the bare metal. The goal is to layer the paint in the chip until it is as thick as the original coat. Try not to get the touch-up on the edges of the chip. If the touch-up paint overlaps the original paint, it will darken it. Good luck with this. It's very difficult to get it perfect. Think of chips in your bicycle as marks of character. The important thing is to cover exposed metal so it won't rust.

Waxing the Bike

The paint finish will last longest if it is protected with wax. Automobile waxes work well on most bicycle paints. If you have a custom bike with a superior quality paint job, you should use a special wax for your paint. Ask for a bicycle wax called *Bike Elixir*. This wax is specially designed for the quality paint jobs found on custom, hand-painted bicycles and will help prevent paint chips and keep the color like new.

Waxes prevent rust on chrome plated parts. Don't waste your good wax for this purpose; use the less expensive car wax instead. Aluminum parts can be waxed also if you want, but it is unnecessary because aluminum parts are anodized at the factory and will continue looking good with an occasional polishing with a soft cloth. Anodization is a protective coat on aluminum. Some folks like the way polishing compounds make aluminum components shine, but it's not a good way to deal with aluminum parts, unless you like polishing your bike all the time. The problem is that when you polish parts with such compounds, you will cut through the anodizing, making it necessary to continue polishing the part with more polish to shine it up when it gets tarnished again. It gets tarnished quicker than it should once the anodization is worn down.

Washing the Bike

The bicycle should not be washed like a car. You don't go down to the corner car wash, plug the machine with a pocket full of quarters and blast the dirt off with a high pressure stream of water. It's fine to do that If you plan to disassemble the entire bike and re-lubricate all the components, but it's the wrong thing to do if you want to ride the next day.

It's fine to use water to clean the bike, but you must use care to keep the water out of the bearings. If you insist on cleaning your bike with a hose, dribble water from above after you have washed off the dirt and grime with a wet rag. Trickle the water over the frame to take away excess dirt and soap suds, but keep it away from the bearings of hubs, bottom bracket, headset and pedals. It's fine for the water to get on these parts. What you want to avoid is the water getting inside the parts and washing out the grease. This is what happens when the water is blasted into the parts from the side; that's why it's important to only dribble the water from the top. If the chain and the sprockets are very greasy and grimy, it's best to remove the whole works and clean them in solvent. I will explain that procedure in Chapter 9, *Brake and Gear Repairs*

7. Bicycle Security

Part of caring for a bicycle is protecting it from the thieves of the world. Bicycles are a good money maker for the professional thief and entertainment for the delinquent. If you leave your bike unlocked often enough, you're going to lose it.

Professional Thieves

There are two types of bicycle thieves that could strip you of your prized possession. The professional thief is in business to steal bikes to resell them and make a quick profit. The pros hunt for good selling models and stake out the area when they find one. Usually they work with accomplices and frequent colleges, parks, transit centers and other locations where they can nab lots of quality bicycles in one stop.

It doesn't matter to the pro if a bike is locked, unless the lock is a foolproof model, usually the U-type. The professional carries bolt cutters to cut padlocks, freon to break chains and electric hacksaws to go through cables. He takes the bikes with the easiest locks to cut, incidentally collecting any unlocked bikes along the way. He then takes the bikes to the next county or city and turns them over to salesmen or sells them outright for very reasonable prices.

Preventing Theft

Professional thieves can be thwarted by leaving the bicycle in different inconspicuous locations. If a bike is locked to the same post long enough, sooner or later someone is going to get the tools, come back and steal the bike. You can prevent this by moving the bike around often. Taking the bicycle with you is another deterrent. Not every store will permit this, but many do.

At restaurants, park and lock the bicycle outside where you can watch it while eating. At home, always bring the bicycle inside and not just in the shed or garage. Lots of bikes have been stolen off porches and out of garages because the owner felt they were safe and neglected to lock them. Even a bike locked in the garage is not as safe as a bicycle put away inside the home. All it takes for it to be stolen is someone to know it's there. For example, the paper boy brings a friend on his route one day. The friend spots the bike in the garage and returns to steal it. An expensive bicycle can be quite tempting.

Amateur Thieves

The joy ride type of thief is the other bike heister. These troublemakers don't even want the bicycle. They just want the thrill of stealing it and abusing it before disposing of it in the river, in the ocean or on a vacant lot. These delinquents ruin the bicycle and dump it, never knowing or caring what type or quality it is.

This type of operator is not apt to choose a locked bike for his mark. Usually he will select a bike on impulse, hop on and ride away. These are the people responsible for the disappearing bike trick: " I just went in to buy a paper, and when I came out thirty seconds later, the bike was gone!" Unlocked bikes are fun for these crooks to steal. Buy a lock and use it.

U-Locks

Using a lock whenever you leave the bike anywhere, and alternating where you leave the bike, greatly reduces chances that it will be stolen. As far as locks go, U-style locks, when used properly, offer the best protection. These locks comprise a bar of steel treated to withstand anything the thief might use to try to cut it. The steel bar is bent into a U shape and has a cross piece that slides over the U and locks onto it. The U locks are used by removing the bicycle's front wheel

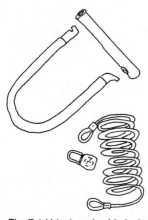

Fig. 7.1 U-lock and cable lock

and putting it next to the rear wheel, passing the lock around both wheels, the frame of the bike and a signpost or some other immovable object, then putting the bar on.

The U-lock is covered with a plastic coating to prevent scratching the frame. It can be carried in a holder on the frame when not in use. Certain brands of U-locks come with a guarantee that pays you money if your bicycle is stolen due to a fault with the lock. Using a U-lock is as close to a guarantee of security for the bicycle as you can get. When you buy a U-lock, make sure you read and save the directions for getting replacement keys, so if you lock your bike and can't find the key, you'll know the proper procedure for getting a new key. Even so, be careful not to lose the key, or your bike will be out of commission until you send for and receive a new key. Don't rely on the bicycle shop to help in this department; they may not sell that brand U-lock any more!

The New York Method

At one time U-locks were considered impregnable, but lately thieves in New York have devised a way to break these locks. The method involves using some pretty heavy equipment and quite often damages the frame of the bike. Some companies now produce special heavy-duty U-locks for high-crime areas like New York to stop this practice. An alternative is to use several types of locks. The longer it takes the thief to get through your protective measures, the more risk of being caught in the act. If you live in a high-crime area, you should definitely select the best lock; in some other places you may be able to get by with other types of locks.

Coil Locks

Some riders prefer not to buy a U-lock. These things are two to three times the price of a cable lock and heavier. They offer superior protection for your bicycle, but in some instances you may prefer a cable lock. The cable lock consists of a six foot vinyl-coated steel cable and a padlock that locks the ends of the cable together.

Self coiling cables are the easiest to carry. They wrap into a small coil automatically when not in use and can be locked under the seat or, better, in a seat or handle-bar bag. When carrying a cable type lock, never wind the cable around the seat post or the frame. The lock will swing around as you ride and continually hit the

frame, chipping the paint severely. If you don't have a
bike bag to put the cable in, lock the cable to the seat
rail under the seat. In this position, the lock might rattle
a bit but it will not hit the frame.

Cable Lock Use

With cables it's not necessary to remove the front
wheel, because the cable will stretch around it. Coil
cables are long enough to wrap around a large tree or
two bikes, if required. There are advantages to coil
cables, but they do not offer the security of a U-lock.
No matter how thick the cable is, it's easy for a person
with an electric hacksaw to buzz through the cable or
with bolt cutters to snip the lock.

If you decide a cable lock is for you, remember to
leave the bike in a location you can watch, and move
it from time to time. The cable is primarily a deterrent.
It's a safe bet that a joy ride thief will leave the bike
alone because it is locked, however a professional thief
could still steal it. You're gambling that the pro will not
spot your bike.

Keeping Accessories Safe

When locking the bicycle, it's smart to take accessories
that aren't bolted to the bike with you, or lock them too.
Pumps, lights, bike bags and other goodies are fair

game to someone looking for parts for his bike.

Many mountain bikes and cruisers come with quick-release seat posts. It's simple for a thief to open the quick-release, and steal the seat unless it too is locked. One way to secure the seat and the seat post to the frame is with a *Seat Leash*. This is a little cable with two loops on the ends that you can buy in many bike shops. One end is put around the frame and the other around the seat. In order to steal the seat, the thief will need the right tools to take the thing apart and the time to use them.

There are also people who get a kick out of vandalizing bicycles. Sometimes this is because they could not successfully steal the bike. Outraged, they smash the bicycle or kick the spokes in on the wheels. There's not much you can do about this type of jerk.

Fooling the Crook

There are ways to slow up a criminal if you have to leave the bike outside temporarily unlocked. One approach is to lock the front brake on by wrapping a rubber band around the front brake lever. Carry a strong elastic with you, or keep it wrapped around the handlebars. When the bike is parked, just compress the brake

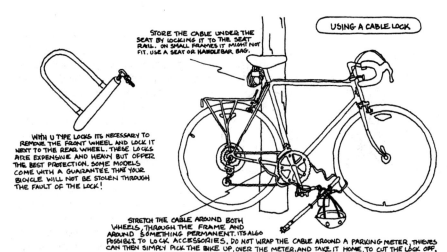

STORE THE CABLE UNDER THE SEAT BY LOCKING IT TO THE SEAT RAIL. ON SMALL FRAMES IT MIGHT NOT FIT. USE A SEAT OR HANDLEBAR BAG.

WITH U TYPE LOCKS ITS NECESSARY TO REMOVE THE FRONT WHEEL AND LOCK IT NEXT TO THE REAR WHEEL. THESE LOCKS ARE EXPENSIVE AND HEAVY BUT OFFER THE BEST PROTECTION. SOME MODELS COME WITH A GUARANTEE THAT YOUR BICYCLE WILL NOT BE STOLEN THROUGH THE FAULT OF THE LOCK!

STRETCH THE CABLE AROUND BOTH WHEELS, THROUGH THE FRAME AND AROUND SOMETHING PERMANENT. ITS ALSO POSSIBLE TO LOCK ACCESSORIES. DO NOT WRAP THE CABLE AROUND A PARKING METER, THIEVES CAN THEN SIMPLY PICK THE BIKE UP, OVER THE METER, AND TAKE IT HOME, TO CUT THE LOCK OFF.

Fig. 7.2 Securing bike and accessories

lever and stretch the elastic around it. Anyone trying to run off with the bike or ride it will discover that it won't roll, and have to carry it. Of course, they could throw the bike in their trunk but that would take more time. Some riders like to carry a wood or plastic wedge and

Fig. 7.3 The clunker

insert this in the lever to lock the front brake. Besides surprising thieves, the locking front brake will prevent the bike from rolling and help it stand parked without moving and falling over.

If your bike has quick-release wheels, you can open the quick-release or remove the front wheel and take it in with you. A bike missing a front wheel looks like a broken down wreck even if it's a nice bicycle. If you merely open the quick-release, the potential jail bird might crash trying to run and jump on the bike because the front wheel will fall off. If you open the rear quick-release, the rear wheel will pull out of the frame when a thief tries to ride the bike away. Although these measures provide no guarantee that your bike will be safe, they will buy you a little time if you ever have to leave your bike unlocked.

Clunkers

As an alternative to leaving your new bike outside and worrying about it, you might decide to get a clunker bike to do errands on. Some cyclists save their good bike for serious riding and get a wreck for around town. Sometimes you can get decent around-town bikes from a shop with a good selection of used bicycles, or you might have a candidate in the garage. An old bike that hasn't seen use in years can often be fixed up to serve as a clunker for around town transportation. Yes, even clunkers get stolen occasionally, but they're much less desirable to a thief, and not worth the risk. Even if it is stolen, at least you're not losing much.

Recovering a Stolen Bike

Having a bicycle stolen is a traumatic experience, but there is a chance that you can get it back. If the bike was registered with the town and had a license, immediately alert the police that it was stolen. Then write a notice as artistically as you can. Offer a reward for the return of the bike. Mention every detail of the bike. Make five hundred copies of the notice and plaster the town with them. Put them up at colleges, high pedestrian traffic areas, telephone poles, restaurants, movie theaters etc. Any place people stand in line is a good place to post them.

Visit every bike shop in the area, and give the flyer to mechanics and the manager to post in the shop or

Fig. 7.4 Publicity to recover stolen bike

put in their stolen bike file. If the bike has special equipment, mention it to the mechanics, so they will have a better chance to identify it if the bike comes into the shop. If your rims are red and the rear tire was bald, tell the mechanics. If someone comes into the shop to buy a rear tire and brings in a wheel with a red rim, an alert sales person will make an effort to locate the bike if there is a reason to be suspicious.

It's easy to get discouraged when your prized possession is stolen, but there is a chance of recovering it if you act fast. You will not get the bike back if you simply call the police with the license and serial number. The police have too much to do to keep track of all the bikes that get stolen or abandoned. They can help to a degree, but don't sit back and expect them to find your bike: they won't. You have to find it, using every resource you have.

8. Tire and Wheel Repairs

Ninety percent of the time, if you maintain your bike, it will remain troublefree. With a little lube now and then, some air in the tires, using care when riding over road hazards, your bike will last a long time. All the same, it is good to know how to perform some simple repairs, just in case something malfunctions on the road.

Flat Tire Repair

The most common thing to go wrong on a bike ride is a flat tire. Anyone riding any further than he'd enjoy walking had better be able to fix a flat. Flat tires can have many causes, and it's practically impossible to avoid getting one sooner or later.

Once in a while you'll ride over a staple or a tack, and immediately lose all the air out of the tire. However, most flats are caused by pieces of glass. The glass sticks to the tire when you ride over it. Usually it does not get through the tire immediately, Instead, it only punctures the tube after you've rolled over it many times. The glass is stuck to the tire and as you ride, it gets pushed further and further, until it eventually cuts through the tire, puncturing the tube. It's not easy to ride with a flat tire and very bad for the wheel to do so. To get home, fixing the flat is the answer, and it's actually quite easy with a little practice and the correct tools.

Even if you avoid every patch of glass and every sharp object visible, you can still get flats. There are thorns from plants that puncture tires and tubes, and small parts that fall off cars, and pieces of wire. No matter how lucky you are, if you ride your bike, you'll get a flat tire now and then. So you should be prepared to deal with it.

Basic Procedure and Tools

To repair a flat, you have to remove the wheel from the bicycle, strip the tire and tube off the wheel, find the hole in the tube, patch the hole (or you can carry a new tube and patch the old one later), remove the sharp object if it is still embedded in the tire, install the tire and tube on the wheel, pump it up and put the wheel back on the bike.

It takes some tools to do all this, and these will be the foundation of your tool kit. What you need is the following: two or three tire levers, a patch kit, a wrench to remove your wheels if they are bolted on, some booting material to patch tire cuts, and a pump.

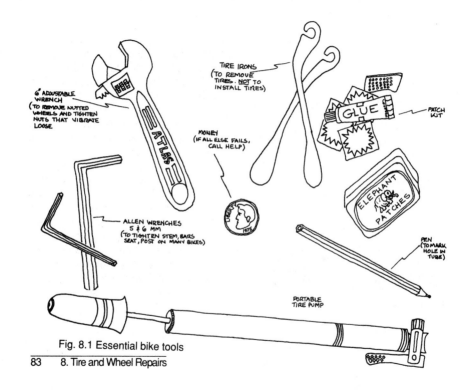

6" ADJUSTABLE WRENCH
(TO REMOVE NUTTED WHEELS AND TIGHTEN NUTS THAT VIBRATE LOOSE.

TIRE IRONS
(TO REMOVE TIRES. NOT TO INSTALL TIRES)

MONEY
(IF ALL ELSE FAILS, CALL HELP)

PATCH KIT

GLUE

ELEPHANT PATCHES

ALLEN WRENCHES
5 & 6 MM
(TO TIGHTEN STEM, EARS SEAT, POST ON MANY BIKES)

PEN
(TO MARK HOLE IN TUBE)

PORTABLE TIRE PUMP

ATLAS

LIBERTY
1975

Fig. 8.1 Essential bike tools

Quick-Release Wheels

Many bicycle wheel hubs come with a mechanism called *quick-release* that allows the wheel to be removed without tools. Instead of axle nuts, the quick-release hub has a lever on one side that loosens or tightens the wheel on the frame when it is twisted from side to side (sometimes marked as *open* and *closed* positions, respectively). If your bicycle has quick-release wheels, you can remove the wheel by hand. Study the illustration, so you are familiar with quick-release operation. If you have any trouble understanding how they function, ask a mechanic at a bike shop to give you a demonstration. If they are not used correctly, the wheels can come out of the frame while riding, so you should know how to use them.

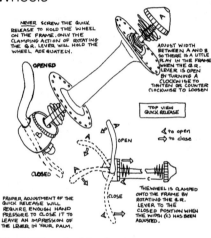

NEVER SCREW THE QUICK RELEASE TO HOLD THE WHEEL ON THE FRAME, ONLY THE CLAMPING ACTION OF ROTATING THE Q.R. LEVER WILL HOLD THE WHEEL ADEQUATELY.

OPENED

ADJUST WIDTH BETWEEN A AND B SO THERE IS A LITTLE PLAY IN THE FRAME WHEN THE Q.R. LEVER IS OPEN BY TURNING A CLOCKWISE TO TIGHTEN OR COUNTER CLOCKWISE TO LOOSEN

TOP VIEW QUICK RELEASE

◁ to open
⇨ to close

OPEN

CLOSED

PROPER ADJUSTMENT OF THE QUICK RELEASE WILL REQUIRE ENOUGH HAND PRESSURE TO CLOSE IT TO LEAVE AN IMPRESSION OF THE LEVER IN YOUR PALM.

CLOSE

THE WHEEL IS CLAMPED ONTO THE FRAME BY ROTATING THE Q.R. LEVER TO THE CLOSED POSITION WHEN THE WIDTH (C) HAS BEEN ADJUSTED.

Fig. 8.2 Use of quick-release

Bolt-on Wheels

If your bike has wheels held on by axles with nuts, it's necessary to use a wrench to remove them. Axle nuts are turned counterclockwise to loosen and clockwise to tighten. Remember: *righty, tighty; lefty, loosey.* The best tool to carry to remove and tighten bolt-on wheels is a six or eight inch long adjustable wrench. With this tool you can also tighten many other things that might loosen up on a ride as well.

Brake Quick-Release

The brake sometimes interferes with the wheel when removing and installing it. The brake is adjusted to be close to the rim, and the tire is usually fatter than the rim. When the tire is flat, it will fit through the brake easily, but when you try to install the wheel with the tire pumped up, it can be impossible to get it through between the brake pads. On some bikes you have to install the wheel with the tire deflated and pump it up later. On most bikes, however, there is an easier way to deal with getting past the brake pads.

To help make wheel removal easy, many bikes have brakes equipped with a quick-release mechanism that loosens the brake adjustment. This should not be confused with the wheel quick-release. The brake quick-release allows you to loosen the brake, so the brake shoes move away from the rim and make more room

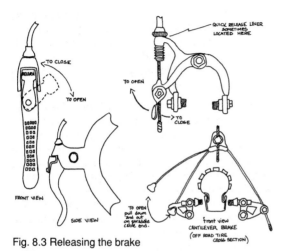

Fig. 8.3 Releasing the brake

for an inflated tire to fit through. The brake quick-release may be located on the brake lever, the brake cable hanger or the brake mechanism itself. You can find it by looking at your brake system closely.

On the brake lever, the quick-release is a movable piece on the front that moves to per- mit the lever to open wider. Brake cable hanger quick-releases are easy to spot. They are attached to the bicycle, not to the brake, usually near the seat post bolt and the upper headset. Quick- releases on the brake itself are little levers near where the end of the brake cable is bolted to the brake.

Mountain Bike Brakes

On many mountain bikes the brake is released by disconnecting the transverse cable, the short one between the two parts of the brake. To open the brake, unhook one side of the cable that runs over the tire to each side of the brake. To do this, hold the shoes to the rim by squeezing them together with one hand, and then pull the end of the cable with the nipple on it down and out. With the transverse cable unhooked, it is very easy to get a large knobby tire through the brake.

Brake quick-releases are nice to help get a wheel off the bike easily, but they have another use too. If you hit a bad hole or crash your bike, you can damage a wheel. When wheels take enough abuse they warp, and warped wheels do not clear closely adjusted brakes. Opening the quick-release on the brake will make more space for the wobbly wheel as it spins, sometimes making it possible to ride home even with a warped wheel.

Wheel Removal

The front wheel is easy to remove from the bicycle. It's a matter of opening the brake quick-release, if you have one, and loosening the front axle nuts or front wheel quick-release. The wheel will drop out when you lift the

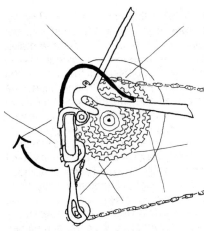

Fig. 8.4 Rotate derailleur back to remove rear wheel

bike. Rear wheels are almost as easy to remove — if you remember a few things.

The rear wheel has a cluster of gears on it and looks like it is attached to the rear derailleur. It looks more complicated than it is. Before removing the rear wheel, shift the chain onto the smallest rear sprocket. To do this, just lift the rear wheel off the ground and pedal the bike. Move the shift lever to change the chain onto the smallest rear sprocket while you pedal. If necessary, open the brake quick-release.

Next, loosen the axle nuts or the wheel quick-release lever. To remove the rear wheel, grab the rear derailleur and pivot it back. Rear derailleurs are designed to do this to get the rear wheel on and off. When the derailleur is pivoted back, the wheel can drop out just like the front wheel. If the chain gets in the way, just wiggle the wheel free of it. If you look at the wheel, you'll notice that the freewheel (cluster of sprockets attached to the the rear wheel hub) is part of the rear wheel. The derailleur is attached to the frame. There's no need to worry about either of these when removing the rear wheel. You can't ruin the shifting of the bike by removing the rear wheel.

Complications

There's one problem you might run into removing the rear wheel, but it's easy to handle if you're ready for it. Some bikes have rear derailleurs that are attached to the frame by an adaptor plate that clamps the rear derailleur into the drop-out (the slot in the back of the frame that the wheel axle fits into). Such an adaptor-mounted derailleur is recognizable by a little nut or screw next to the right hand rear axle nut or quick-release. Before removing the rear wheel, look closely at the rear derailleur for this nut. The derailleur is attached to a plate that

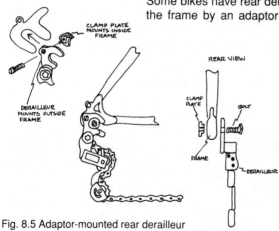

Fig. 8.5 Adaptor-mounted rear derailleur

fits next to the outside of the axle slot (drop-out) of the frame. To hold the derailleur in place, there is a back-up plate inside the drop-out. The bolt passes through the outer plate and screws into the inner plate, holding the derailleur in place by pinching the frame.

Occasionally this type of derailleur will fall off with the wheel when repairing a rear flat. This can be prevented by checking the nut for tightness before removing the wheel. If you forget, and the derailleur falls out of the frame, it's just a matter of putting it back in place and tightening the bolt. Remember to put the adaptor plate on the *outside* and the backup plate *inside* the drop-out. Slide it back until it stops, and tighten the bolt securely, so it stays put next time.

Tire Removal

With the wheel off the bike, all you have to do to repair the flat tire is remove the tire and the tube, find the hole and patch it. Lightweight bicycle tires fit tightly on the rim (mountain bike tires fit more loosely). To get a tight-fitting tire off, you have to use tire levers, also referred to as tire irons. Never use a screwdriver to get the tire off the rim, because it will puncture the tube with its sharp edges. Tire levers are essential tools for your tool kit. They have rounded edges that help pry a tire off the rim. They are not used to put a tire on, only to *remove* it. Use two or three tire levers to remove the tire.

Using Tire Levers

Start removing the tire by putting one tire lever under the tire and prying a little section of the tire up directly across from the valve stem and leaving it there. You can hook the other end of the tire lever to a spoke or hold it with your hand. Now use another tire lever. Put it three or four inches away from the first one and lift another section of the tire up. Use the third tire lever to go a little further and then take out the first one and move it further. After you've done this a few times, you can pull one side of the tire off the rim by hand all the way around.

When one side of the tire is completely off the rim, reach inside the tire opposite the valve stem and grab the tube. Pull it out as far as it will go. The tube will only come out seven eighths of the way because the valve stem, which is attached to the tube, passes through the rim. Unless the tire is a very loose fit, It won't come out of the tire until the tire is completely off the rim. Now you

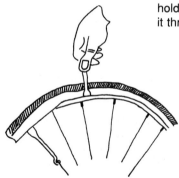

Fig. 8.6 Using tire levers to remove

Valve Types and Pumps

Fig. 8.7
Presta and Schraeder valves

can wiggle the valve stem out and inspect the tube to find the hole.

To find the puncture in the tube, pump it up. Air is put into the tube at the valve. Two types of valves are common on bicycle tubes: Schraeder and Presta. Your pump should match your valve. Schraeder valves are the same type used on cars. Presta valves are unique to bicycles. The Presta, sometimes called 'French' or 'needle' valve, has a smaller diameter and a different end than a Schraeder. On the Schraeder valve you just attach the pump, but on a Presta it's necessary to unscrew the very top of the valve to put air in or let air ou.t I'm assuming that you've already removed the plastic valve cap — these caps are more decoration than anything else.

Presta valves can be changed to fit Schraeder pumps with a small screw-on or press-on adapter. Schraeder valves are not as easily adapted, so it's best to get the correct pump for this valve.

Finding the Hole

Inflate the tube until it is completely rounded out. If you can't put air in the tube, there is a big hole somewhere that should be easy to find. With air in the tube, you can hear air leaking out and follow the noise to the hole. Sometimes the tube doesn't seem to be losing air. You can't hear it, you can't see it, and the tube isn't shrinking. It's time to put the tube under water. If you're working at home, you can fill up the sink with water, but on a ride you usually put in a new tube and patch the old one at home. If you're touring and have a mess kit, it's possible to fill up a pot with water to put the tube in, one little section at a time, to find the hole.

Slow Leaks

Once in a while, with a Schraeder valve, the hole is not detectable even under water. In that case, put the valve under the water and watch it for a couple of minutes non-stop. Slow leaks can develop at the valve stem if the valve core loosens up. This would be a very slow leak. To fix a leaky valve requires a valve core tightener which your local bike shop or any garage will let you use if they don't have one for sale.

When the tire has a very slow leak, you can save yourself a lot of trouble by checking the valve before taking the wheel off the bike. Just put some saliva on the valve (with the tire fully inflated) and watch for the leak. It will show up as bubbles on the top of the valve. If it leaks, tighten the valve core and check it again by putting more saliva on top of the valve. If tightening the valve doesn't do the trick, and you are sure it is leaking, try removing the valve and putting a drop of oil on the valve core before replacing it. This will often stop a valve leak.

Patching the Hole

Mark the hole in the tube when you find it. There are a couple of ways to do this. One of the easiest is to make the hole bigger by putting something in the hole and tearing it open a bit. This will make it simple to keep track of the hole once the glue is on it and will still be simple to patch. Another method is to mark the hole with a pen. Put your marks well away from the hole, so you can see them when you go to put the patch on. If you put your marks too close to the hole, the glue will cover them, making them invisible. Put two marks, one beside and one above the hole, well outside the area to receive the glue.

Patch Kits

A good patch kit is a must for your tool kit. Patches that bond with the tube are called self-vulcanizing. They patch holes best. *Rema*, *Tip Top* and *Specialized* are brands that work well. Besides patches, the patch kit contains rubber solution (adhesive), a rubber buffer (usually sandpaper), and sometimes a small rubber wand to apply glue to the tube.

The area to be patched has to be roughed up to produce a good bond. Use the sandpaper or metal buffer in the patch kit and buff the surface at and around the hole. The tube of rubber solution in the patch kit, when new, will have a lead seal on the end to prevent leaking. To puncture this seal, most glue tubes have a double screw-on cap: the inside of the cap contains a spike to puncture the tube. Remove this cap, invert it, and press the spike into the seal.

Put adhesive on the hole and spread it out over an area slightly larger than the patch to be used. It's possible to patch quite large holes, so don't hesitate to try fixing even gashes three quarters of an inch long. Put plenty of adhesive on, and go on to the next step. The longer the adhesive sets on the tube, the better the bond. Wait five minutes at least. The patch should not be applied until the glue is completely dry.

Checking the Tire

While the glue is drying, check the tire. Try to find the object that popped the tube. One effective way to do this is to run a rag around the inside of the tire. Be sure to do this in both directions. The rag will snag on anything that could have punctured the tube. Work at this, because nothing is more frustrating than to get the flat repaired only to have another puncture immediately afterwards, because there was still something in the tire. You may find that there is nothing inside the tire at all. This means that whatever caused the flat went through, but didn't stay in the tire. In any case, don't put the tire back on until you're sure there is nothing left in it that could puncture the tube again.

Before putting the patch on, be certain the glue is dry. The directions in most patch kits recommend testing the glue with the back of the hand. It's OK to put the patch on If the glue is not sticky any more. Use whatever method you want, but don't rush it. Good patch bonds occur only if the glue dries adequately.

Patches

Quality patches are sandwiched between a layer of cellophane and a layer of foil (cheap patches just have a backing over the glued surface of the patch). The foil covers the sticky part of the patch and the cellophane covers the top of the patch, giving you something to hold onto. Sometimes you have to be careful when peeling the foil off the patch, to make sure the patch doesn't come off with the foil. The idea is to remove the foil, leaving the patch stuck to the cellophane. Then you can apply it over the hole in the tube, holding on to the patch by the cellophane.

Once the patch is in place, it's not necessary to remove the cellophane, but some folks like to peel it off to test the bond between the patch and the tube. Once you've got the patch in place on the hole in the tube, roll something over it a few times to knead it into the tube securely. The end of a frame type pump works well.

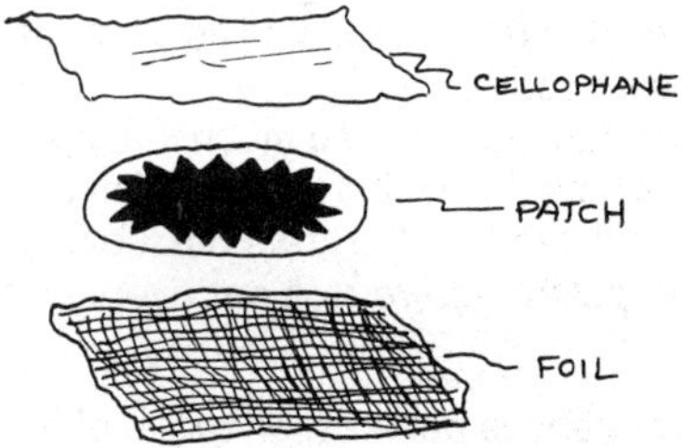

CELLOPHANE

PATCH

FOIL

Fig. 8.8 Tire patch

Spare Tubes

On a ride, it's easiest to carry a good spare tube in your tool kit. In the event of a flat, you remove the punctured tube and install the spare. If you get a flat on a rainy day, it's no fun trying to find the hole in the tube and waiting for the glue to dry. Spare tubes save time and prevent inconvenience. After the ride, you can patch the punctured tube and put that in your kit as the spare.

Patching Tires

Tires can also be patched. The average bicycle tire should last from one thousand to three thousand miles, depending on the weight of the rider and gear and the conditions it is used for. Tires are not inexpensive either, so it's worth using them as long as possible. A frugal cyclist will ride a tire until it's as bald as a marble and the thread shows through.

Bad glass cuts can damage a tire so much that it will no longer contain the tube. When the tube is inflated, it will bulge out through the hole in the tire. With the right equipment, you can patch the tire and get every last mile out of it.

Tire Booting

Carry a few denim or canvas patches, or boots, of assorted sizes in your tool kit. Saturate these patches in rubber cement, and put them in a small plastic bag when they have dried. Sprinkle a little talcum powder In another plastic bag,. Carry these with your regular tube patch kit, and even bad tire cuts will not stop you.

Use the tire patches inside the tire over a cut. Put the same adhesive in the patch kit over the tire cut on the inside and some on one side of the tire patch. This new adhesive will freshen the rubber cement you had put on before. Wait for it to dry on both surfaces, and put the patch over the cut. To finish the job, sprinkle talcum powder over the patch, so the excess adhesive on the tire won't stick to the tube. Pumped up to maximum pressure, a patched tire might bulge at the tire cut, but it will last and let you ride many more miles.

Installing Tire and Tube

Start putting the tire and the tube on the rim by pumping up the tube until it just takes shape. Put the rounded-out tube inside the tire. Holding the tire with the tube inside it, start putting it on the wheel. Use the floor to help. Lay the wheel on the floor and put the tire on top of it. Line the valve up with the valve hole in the rim and put the valve in with a small section of one side of the tire on the rim. Do not pull the valve stem all the way into the rim.

The tire has two wire beads inside it. These are metal-wire hoops that are enclosed in channels on either edge of the tire. These beads give the tire its shape and prevent it from blowing off the rim when fully inflated. The beads have to be under the tube all the way around the wheel. If the tube or the valve gets under the beads of the tire, the tube will lift the tire, bulging the sidewall and causing a hop in the tire when you inflate it.

Put the rest of one side of the tire on with your fingers. It will be difficult to put the tire on If there is too much air in the tube. Let a little air out at a time until you can get one side of the tire on. The tube should not be completely deflated at this point. It's too easy to trap the tube under the bead if it's completely flat, so let out a little air and keep trying.

With one side of the tire in place, work the tube onto the rim and inside the tire all the way around. Now one side of the tire is on the rim, and the tube is slightly inflated inside the tire and on the rim.

Starting at the valve stem again, work the other side of the tire onto the rim. Use both hands simultaneously in opposite directions around the wheel. As you start, be careful again not to trap the valve stem under the tire bead. To accomplish this, push the valve stem up inside the tire as you put on the other bead. Then con-

Putting on the Last Section

tinue installing the tire. Put a small section at a time on with each hand working away from the other.

It will get difficult to put the bead on as your hands start moving in towards each other at the top of the wheel. At this point, let the air out of the tube and, instead of trying to push the tire on with the fingers, roll this tight portion on with the palms or heels of your hands.

Hold your hand on one side of this last section where the tire is partially on and partially off the rim, keeping it there. With your other hand, gradually roll the last portion of the tire bead onto the rim a little bit at a time. Concentrate on putting the final portion of the tire on one inch at a time. It helps to put the wheel on a table or bench to support it and use some body English to put the bead on all the way. Once you've put a tire on by hand and you see how it's done, you'll be able to do it again. If you simply cannot master the procedure, ask the mechanic at your local bike shop to demonstrate the procedure for you.

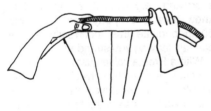

Fig. 8.9 Rolling last section of tire on

It's mostly technique and experience that allows bicycle mechanics to make this look easy. Practice will help. Regardless of how tight the tire is, do not pry it on with tire levers or anything else, because you'll just pop the tube again.

Pump Use

Pumping the tire up with a good floor pump is easy. You can support the pump by standing on its base and inflate the tire with both hands on the handle of the plunger. It's a different story with a frame pump that you carry on the bike.

The frame pump is very small compared to the floor pump. It is designed to fit on the bike, to be used primarily in an emergency. Because it is short and very light, it is important to know how to properly use the frame pump to inflate tires. Incorrectly used, it can fail, leaving you stranded.

With a Presta valve, just remember to unscrew the tip of the valve. You can't put air into the Presta valve unless this tip is unscrewed. It also helps to push the tip down before attempting to put air in the

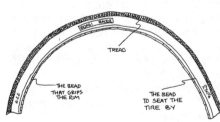

TREAD

THE BEAD THAT GRIPS THE RIM

THE BEAD TO SEAT THE TIRE BY

Fig. 8.10 Tire bead and centering marker

tube. This breaks the seal in the valve. If you forget to do this, you may have trouble putting air in the valve. With a Schraeder valve, you simply put the pump on and inflate the tube.

Frame Pump Use

To pump up the tires with the frame pump, attach the valve fitting onto the valve with the valve in a convenient position. I like to put the wheel so the valve is near the top. Some *Zéfal* pumps have a small locking tab that locks the pump on the valve when it is flipped up. Most other pumps rely on a press fit to hold the pump on the valve.

Once the pump is on the valve, you can inflate the tire. Do not just grab both ends of the pump and start pumping. If you don't give the pump some support at the valve stem, it's likely you'll pull the valve out of the tube or break it. To support the valve, wrap your index finger around a spoke and your thumb up, over the tire. The remaining fingers should be wrapped tightly around the end of the pump.

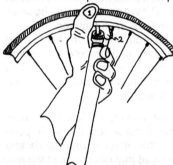

SUPPORTING THE VALVE
STEM
1 PUT THUMB OVER TOP OF TIRE
2 WRAP INDEX FINGER AROUND SPOKE
Fig. 8.11 Use of frame pump

Inflating the tire takes time with a frame pump. Pump very deliberately one stroke at a time and count to fifty or so. You should be pushing the plunger in with your stronger arm. Use your shoulder to help fully inflate the tire by leaning into each stroke.

With a pressure gauge, it's easy to check how much air is in the tire. If you don't have one, squeeze the other tire to get a feel for how much air is required.

To remove the pump from the valve, loosen the thumb tab lock, if there is one, and then knock the pump straight down with a sharp blow from your palm. The idea is not to wiggle the pump, which could pull out the valve, but to knock it off straight.

Inflating the Tube

When you're fixing a flat, use care inflating the tube. Put a little air in at first to check how the tire is positioned on the rim. Spin the wheel in your hands and look at the edge of the bead that sits on top of the rim. There is a small rubber line just above the enclosed wire bead on all tires. This line is on the tire to help you put it on the rim straight. When spinning the wheel, look at the line. The line should be visible all around as the wheel rotates on both sides of the wheel. Look for any inconsistency.

If the line dips under the rim or jumps way above the rim, let the air out and check the spots where the flaws were. When the line jumps above the rim, it is an indication that the tube is trapped under the bead. With air in the tube, it lifts the tire off the rim. When the tire line dips as the wheel spins, it is because the bead is stuck below the rim edge. Sometimes pumping the tire up to a higher pressure will get the bead out. You can also let the air out and put a soapy solution at the bad spot and then pump it up again. Sometimes the slippery soap will help the tire seat correctly. With perseverance almost any tire can be correctly seated on the rim. Some tires are better than others, but all tires run smoothly when put on the rim straight.

Avoiding Punctures

Skilled cyclists practice certain techniques to avoid getting punctures. They watch the road and avoid patches of glass, gravel and other debris. Their tires are regularly inflated to the recommended pressure, and they inspect them regularly to see that there is adequate tread and there are no serious cuts.

A technique that helps prevent flats on ten-speeds is cleaning tires while riding. If you ride through an unavoidable patch of glass, it can help to clean off the tires immediately. It's called *dusting* the tires. The maneuver takes coordination, because it is done while you're riding.

The idea is to reach over the handlebars with one arm and rest your gloved hand gently on the tire to dust off any glass that may have stuck to the tire. To dust off the rear wheel, reach back between the seat tube of the frame and the seat stays, and put your hand on the tire. Be careful not to let the tire pull your hand down and jam it between the frame and tire. These practices will help you prevent flats and extend tire life on lightweight ten-speed bicycles. It is not necessary to dust mountain bike tires. If you feel like it is too difficult to do while riding, simply stop and get off the bike to do clean them whenever you have run over glass.

Front Wheel Installation

Installing the wheel is the last step in fixing a flat tire. The front wheel has to be securely inserted into the fork and tightened. If the wheel is bolted on, make sure there is a washer under the nut, outside the fork blade, before tightening. First merely snug one nut, then the other. Check the wheel in the fork to see that it is centered. You can slide one finger between the rim and fork on both sides to get an idea how well centered it is. If the wheel and fork are perfect, the wheel will center by itself if it is fully inserted in the fork ends. The wheel does not have to be perfectly centered, but it will rub against the brake if it's too far off center. Don't fully tighten the axle nuts until the wheel is reasonably centered. When it is centered, tighten one nut and then the other until the wheel is fastened securely.

Rear Wheel Installation

Installing the rear wheel in the frame takes a bit more effort than the front wheel. Rear wheels are more difficult to center because they have to be centered between both the seat stays and the chain stays. You shouldn't be afraid of the chain and the derailleur if you removed the wheel. The chain was on the small rear sprocket when the wheel was removed, so put it there to install it. If this proves difficult to do, it could be that the shift lever has changed position. Check that the right lever is all the way forward on a ten-speed; on a mountain bike, the thumb shift levers should be all the way back toward the rider.

If Things Get in Your Way

With the chain on the small rear sprocket, you should be able to pull the wheel back into the frame. Remember to pull the derailleur back as you insert the wheel. A few things can make wheel insertion tricky. Put up the kickstand if there is one on the bike. The kickstand won't hit the wheel, but with the chain on the sprocket, the crank arm will move backwards and hit the stand as the wheel is pulled back. This makes it impossible to pull the wheel back into the frame. You avoid this by putting the kickstand up out of the way

The other thing that could make putting the rear wheel on difficult is the axle nuts, washers or quick-release. These parts can interfere when trying to install the wheel. You can remove the axle nuts and washers altogether to make it easier on a bolt-on wheel. On a quick-release wheel, loosening the quick-release lever will make it easier.

Tighten Rear Wheel

When the rear wheel is in place, snug the nuts or quick-release to hold it, and check the centering. Use thumbs on either side of the top of the wheel as a gauge, and check the bottom by eye. Tighten the nuts on both sides gradually as described for the front wheel (one side at a time) when the wheel is centered. Rear axle nuts have to be tightened very securely. The force applied by the leg muscles is enough to pull a loose wheel forward in the frame. Once you are content that the wheel is centered, tighten the axle nuts as tight as you can with the adjustable wrench.

Quick-release wheels also have to be securely fastened. The proper tension requires significant effort to rotate the lever all the way across to the closed position. When the lever is tight enough, it will leave its impression in the palm of your hand from the effort of closing it.

Tighten Brakes

Remember to close the brake quick-release after installing the wheels. On cantilever brakes and U-brakes on cruisers or mountain bikes, be sure to hook up the transverse cable while squeezing the brake arms together against the rim.

9. Brake and Gear Repairs

The Brakes

The safe operation of a bicycle is in large part controlled by the condition of the brakes. Most brakes are fitted with an adjuster that allows adjusting the brakes without tools. This adjustment should be used if the brake shoes are worn down or the brake cable stretched, causing the brakes to work poorly.

Barrel Adjusters

On the road, brake adjustments are done with the brake barrel adjusters. This is a small threaded cylinder that fits on one end of the brake cable. The barrel adjuster is turned counterclockwise to tighten the brake when it feels too loose. You shouldn't have to pull the brake lever too far to apply the brake. Anything more than an inch of brake lever travel means it's time to adjust.

If the brake has an adjuster, it may be on the lever, the brake or the cable anchor. You can find the barrel adjuster by checking these three parts of the brake. Usually the barrel adjuster has a round locknut on it. After backing off the barrel, screw the locknut down to lock the adjustment.

Brake Shoes

When the brakes loosen on a bike without brake barrel adjustments, check the brake shoes. Sometimes you can replace the shoes, and the brakes will work like new again. Brake shoes have slots in them or knobs that help channel water off the rims on rainy days. These shapes on the shoes are the indicators for brake shoe wear: like tread on a car tire. It's time to replace the shoes when the knobs are almost worn flat, or the slots are not deep any more, It helps to look at the brake shoes when they're new to know how much wear they have.

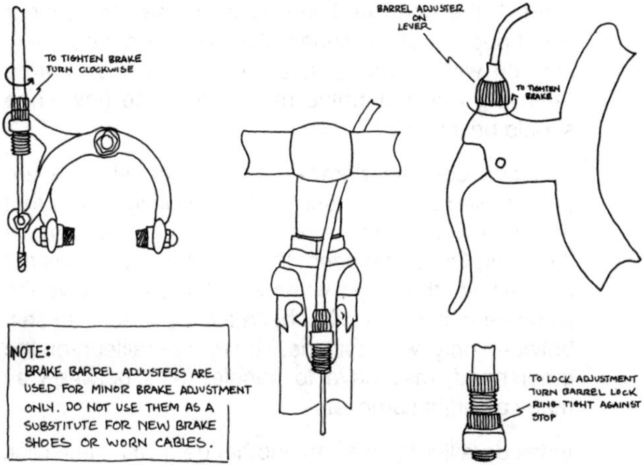

TO TIGHTEN BRAKE TURN CLOCKWISE

BARREL ADJUSTER ON LEVER

TO TIGHTEN BRAKE

TO LOCK ADJUSTMENT TURN BARREL LOCK RING TIGHT AGAINST STOP

NOTE:
BRAKE BARREL ADJUSTERS ARE USED FOR MINOR BRAKE ADJUSTMENT ONLY. DO NOT USE THEM AS A SUBSTITUTE FOR NEW BRAKE SHOES OR WORN CABLES.

Fig. 9.1
Brake barrel adjuster (similar device used on derailleur)

Brake shoes should be installed to match the bevel on the rim and in the correct direction. If the shoe only has one closed end (most brake shoes are closed on both ends), the closed end should be put facing forward. If the open end were put forward, the rubber could pop out of the shoe holder in a hard stop, leaving you without brake. Look at the old shoe before removing it to determine exactly how the new shoe should be installed.

Derailleurs

The most common derailleurs on modern bicycles are the indexed types. These feature clicking levers that automatically select the gear for you when you move the lever. On a ten-speed, the front derailleur does not have a lever that clicks when you shift it. In case you're wondering, it doesn't click because it's so easy to shift between only two positions. The rear derailleur, on the other hand, may have to handle shifts between as many as eight sprockets.

Derailleur Adjustments

Index derailleurs shift into another gear with each click of the shift lever if one condition is met: the cable must be just tight enough to move the derailleur far enough

Fig. 9.2
Rear view of bent derailleur

for it to shift the chain onto the next sprocket with each click of the lever. If the cable is too loose, the derailleur will move when you click the shift lever, but the chain will only move partway to the next sprocket. Sometimes this will create minor problems, like chain noise, but usually a loose cable will allow the chain to slip out of gear. This often happens when you are climbing a hill in a low gear. The bike will suddenly get harder to pedal because the chain jumps onto a smaller sprocket, making it more difficult to climb the hill. This can be very annoying.

The manufacturers of indexed drivetrains expected cables to stretch on their systems, so they built in an adjuster to make it easy for you to adjust your derailleur if this happens. The adjustment is made with an adjustment barrel on the derailleur. If you follow the path of the cable to where it enters the rear derailleur, you'll find a small knurled adjuster at the back of the derailleur. By turning this adjuster counterclockwise (toward the spokes), one half turn at a time, you can increase the tension of the shift cable. In most cases this is all it takes to adjust an index derailleur that is not shifting correctly. Turn the adjuster only a half turn at a time and then try the shifting before you tighten it any more. That way you won't overtighten the cable.

Friction Shifters

Friction derailleurs were designed to operate trouble-free without adjustments. Cable tension also has something to do with how these derailleurs shift, but it is not as critical as it is with index systems. Once friction derailleurs have been adjusted correctly, usually during assembly, they do not have to be readjusted under normal use. The only adjustment you may need is a shift lever adjustment, not a derailleur adjustment. This is true of most front derailleurs on index bikes too. On indexed derailleurs, the clicks in the lever keep the derailleur in gear, so it is not something to worry about on indexed rear derailleurs.

Shift Lever Tension

The derailleurs use springs to help shift. To resist the pull of the derailleur springs, shift levers are tensioned. When shifting, the lever holds the derailleur in position. If the tension on the shift lever is inadequate, the derailleur will shift unintentionally. This is because the shift lever was not tight enough to stay in place, and the derailleur spring's pull on the cable caused the shift lever to move just as if you moved it with your thumb or finger. Such unintentional shifting usually happens when you're climbing a hill in a low gear, because that is when the derailleur spring is stretched to it's maximum and has the most tension. All of a sudden the chain will pop into the next gear, sometimes sending the rider flying.

Look at the sides of the shift levers, or on the top of them on a cruiser or mountain bike. There will be a screw or D-ring on the middle of the lever. This is a screw that allows the rider to adjust the shift lever tension. These screws have to be adjusted occasionally. If the derailleur shifts unintentionally, it's because this screw has loosened up. D-rings can be tightened by hand. Regular screws require a screwdriver. It's usually easy to find something by the roadside to tighten it with if you don't have tools with you when this happens.

Bent Derailleurs

A common derailleur ailment is bending. When the bicycle falls over on the right side, due to a faulty kickstand or an accident, the rear derailleur can be bent inward toward the wheel. This will cause the derailleur to shift too far to the inside and not far enough to the outside. When you try to shift into the lowest gear, the derailleur will rub against the spokes or the spoke guard, and it will hesitate shifting down onto the smallest rear sprocket when you try to shift into high gear.

Get it Straightened

A bicycle mechanic can repair this problem by straightening the bent derailleur. It is not something to be repaired by experimenting with the screws in the back of the derailleur. Those screws are set by the mechanic who assembled your bike, and in most cases they don't need further adjustment. It's easy to cause major problems by experimenting with them if you don't know how they work. They don't change adjustment on their own, so it's best to leave them alone.

10. Conclusion

After purchasing my first bicycle, I made every mistake possible. Assuming that the bicycle was a fairly simple machine, I gave it little thought. I rode with the seat too low, in gears too big. I didn't lubricate the chain and rarely pumped up the tires. I never shifted and rarely cleaned the bike.

How I Learned

I was determined to ride, though, and after several months of practicing bad habits, I got lucky. On my last legs, riding through the White Mountains in New Hampshire, I met Galen Farrington. An accomplished touring cyclist, Galen was on his way to New Mexico. He was riding one hundred miles a day at eighteen miles an hour. His trip was completely organized. Each day he had a planned campsite with an interesting place to visit. He was equipped with a thorough tool kit and knew how to use it.

In contrast, I was riding ten miles an hour. I had no tools, not even a pump or a spare tube. I didn't even have enough money left to buy lunch. I still had eighty miles to go, and I was exhausted.

With tact, Galen explained the deficiency of my riding style. He told me that if I shifted occasionally, I'd save energy. He pointed out that my tires were soft and the derailleurs needed adjusting. He recommended buying some gloves and changing seats.

When he found out I had no money, he bought me lunch. It had been an enlightening experience for me. It encouraged me to seek out other cyclists and learn everything I could about bicycling.

It's Easy to do it Right

I hope that, armed with the information contained in this book, you can avoid most beginners' mistakes. Cycling can be a lot of fun. It shouldn't be necessary to learn about bicycling by doing everything wrong the first time. There's no need to make your own mistakes: learn from mine instead.

About the Author

Jim Langley became interested in bicycles as a teenager, touring in Massachusetts and New Hampshire on an English three-speed. Short trips grew to long tours, three speeds became ten, and in the winter of 1979 he cycled five thousand miles across the US with his wife Deb.

As Jim's passion for the bicycle increased, he sought employment in the bike industry, and in 1971 he took a job in a bike shop. He spent most of the next 19 years working as a mechanic or service manager in shops in New Hampshire, Vermont and California. During this time, he assembled thousands of new bicycles and learned every aspect of bicycle repair. He also taught maintenance courses in shops to customers and at the University of California Santa Cruz, raced on and off road (finishing one national championship), manufactured a bicycle brake tool of his own design, started collecting antique bicycles, and took every opportunity to learn more about his trade by attending numerous industry seminars.

In the early eighties, he began writing technical articles for bicycling publications *California Bicyclist* and *Velo News*. In 1989, he left the bike shop for a full time editorial job with *Bicycling Magazine*. In *The New Bike Book*, he introduces bicycles and cycling to the newcomer, drawing on his personal riding and working experience.

Bibliography

The following lists just a couple of books that are intended for the non-technically inclined bicycle owner. See the bibliographies in any of the titles listed for additional references.

Ballantine, R. *Richard's Bicycle Book*. New York: Ballantine Books, 1979.

Borysewicz, E. *Bicycle Road Racing*. Brattleboro: Velo News, 1985.

Cuthberson, T. *Anybody's Bike Book*. Berkeley: Ten-Speed Press, 1984.

Van der Plas, R. *Roadside Bicycle Repairs*. San Francisco: Bicycle Books, 1990 (2nd Ed).

———. *The Bicycle Commuting Book.*. San Francisco: Bicycle Books, 1989.

———. *The Mountain Bike Book*. San Francisco: Bicycle Books, 1988 (2nd Ed.).

Ritchie, A. *King of the Road*. London: Wildwood House, 1975.

Snowling, S and K. Evans. *Bicycle Mechanics*. Champaign: Leisure Press, 1986.

Index

Book Ordering Form

All books published by Bicycle Books, Inc. may be obtained through the book or bike trade. If not available locally, order directly from the publisher. Allow three weeks for delivery. Fill out both sides of coupon and mail to:

Bicycle Books, Inc.
PO Box 2038
Mill Valley CA 94941 (USA)

Please include payment in full (check or money order payable to Bicycle Books, Inc.).If not paid in advance, books will be sent UPS COD.

Canadian and other foreign customers please note: Prices quoted are in US Dollars. Postage and handling fee for foreign orders is $2.50 per book. Payment in US currency (enquire at your bank) must be enclosed — no COD available.

Sub Total (enter amount from reverse of form): $ _____

California residents add 6.5% tax: $ _____

Shipping and handling $1.50 per book: $ _____

Total amount (pay this amount):   **$** _____

Name: _____

Address: _____

City, state, zip _____ Tel.: (____) _____

Charge to VISA/MC No. _____ Signature _____

Book Ordering Form (please fill out both sides)

☐ Check here if payment enclosed

Please send the following books:

The Mountain Bike Book	___ copies @	$9.95 =	$ _____
The Bicycle Repair Book	___ copies @	$8.95 =	$ _____
The Bicycle Racing Guide	___ copies @	$10.95 =	$ _____
The Bicycle Touring Manual	___ copies @	$10.95 =	$ _____
Roadside Bicycle Repairs	___ copies @	$4.95 =	$ _____
Major Taylor (hardcover)	___ copies @	$19.95 =	$ _____
Bicycling Fuel	___ copies @	$7.95 =	$ _____
Mountain Bike Maintenance	___ copies @	$7.95 =	$ _____
In High Gear (hardcover)	___ copies @	$18.95 =	$ _____
In High Gear (softcover)	___ copies @	$10.95 =	$ _____
The Bicycle Fitness Book	___ copies @	$7.95 =	$ _____
The Bicycle Commuting Book	___ copies @	$7.95 =	$ _____
The New Bike Book	___ copies @	$4.95 =	$ _____
Bicycle Technology	___ copies @	$14.95 =	$ _____

Sub Total (transfer to reverse of form): $ _____

Bicycle Books, Inc., PO Box 2038, Mill Valley CA 94941, Tel. (415) 381 0172